© 2015 by Wayne Unze

ISBN-10: 1507712545

All Rights Reserved. No part of this publication may be reproduced in any form or by any means, including scanning, photocopying, or otherwise without prior written permission of the copyright holder.

First Printing, 2015

Printed in the United States of America

Income Disclaimer

This document contains business strategies, marketing methods and other business advice that, regardless of my own results and experience, may not produce the same results (or any results) for you. I make absolutely no guarantee, expressed or implied, that by following the advice below you will make any money or improve current profits, as there are several factors and variables that come into play regarding any given business.

Primarily, results will depend on the nature of the product or business model, the conditions of the marketplace, the experience of the individual, and situations and elements that are beyond your control.

As with any business endeavor, you assume all risks related to investment and money based on your own discretion and at your own potential expense.

Liability Disclaimer

By reading this document, you assume all risks associated with using the advice given below, with a full understanding that you, solely, are responsible for anything that may occur as a result of putting this information into action in any way, and regardless of your interpretation of the advice.

You further agree that our company cannot be held responsible in any way for the success or failure of your business as a result of the information presented below. It is your responsibility to conduct your own due diligence regarding the safe and successful operation of your business if you intend to apply any of our information in any way to your business operations.

Terms of Use

You are given a nontransferable, "personal use" license to this product. You cannot distribute it or share it with other individuals.

Also, there are no resale rights or private label rights granted when purchasing this document. In other words, it's for your own personal use only.

YOU The Boss

1. How to Go Into Business Without Losing Your Shirt
2. How to Retire In Style

By Wayne J. Unze

TABLE OF CONTENTS

Description   Page

PART ONE: HOW TO GO INTO BUSINESS WITHOUT LOSING YOUR SHIRT 7

Chapter One: An Entrepreneurial Test *10*
Chapter Two: How To Go Into Business (An Overview) *13*
Chapter Three: Starting A Business *15*
Chapter Four: Purchasing An Existing Business Or Franchise *24*
Chapter Five: The Nondisclosure Agreement *28*
Chapter Six: Purchasing A New Franchise *31*
Chapter Seven: Valuing A Business *34*
Chapter Eight: The Abc's Of Financing The Purchase *49*
Chapter Nine: Negotiating An Asset Purchase Agreement *56*
Chapter Ten: Understanding The Asset Purchase Agreement *60*
Chapter Eleven: The Asset Purchase Agreement *70*
Chapter Twelve: The Art Of Due Diligence *77*
Chapter Thirteen: The All-Important Lease *82*
Chapter Fourteen: Commercial Lease Agreement *86*
Chapter Fifteen: The Lease Assignment *93*
Chapter Sixteen: Closing The Sale *95*
Chapter Seventeen: Avoiding The Post-Purchase Blues *98*
Chapter Eighteen: Guerilla Cash Flow Management *102*

PART TWO: HOW TO RETIRE IN STYLE *106*

Introduction *107*
Chapter One: Preparing A Business For Sale *110*
Chapter Two: Valuing A Business *114*
Chapter Three: Cash Vs. Terms *129*
Chapter Four: Selecting The Right Business Broker *133*
Chapter Five: Understanding The Listing Agreement *137*
Chapter Six: Sole And Exclusive Listing Agreement *137*
Chapter Seven: The Nondisclosure Agreement *148*

Chapter Eight: The Selling Process *151*
Chapter Nine: Negotiating An Asset Purchase Agreement *154*
Chapter Ten: Understanding The Asset Purchase Agreement *158*
Chapter Eleven: The Asset Purchase Agreement *168*
Chapter Twelve: The Seller's Role In Due Diligence *175*
Chapter Thirteen: The Catch 22 Of Selling "Cash" Businesses .. *178*
Chapter Fourteen: Earn-Outs *180*
Chapter Fifteen: Retail Businesses - Liquidation Or Sale *182*
Chapter Sixteen: The Seller's Lease Concerns *185*
Chapter Seventeen: Avoid Bidding Wars *191*
Chapter Eighteen: Sell Your Business – Pay No Taxes *193*
Chapter Nineteen: Gifting Your Business To Employees Or Family *195*

Wayne J. Unze
BUSINESS CONSULTANT/APPRAISER
www.you-the-boss.com

PART ONE:
HOW TO GO INTO BUSINESS WITHOUT LOSING YOUR SHIRT

INTRODUCTION

According to a past Fortune magazine article, more than 75 percent of the 400 wealthiest Americans achieved their riches through business ownership. The rest found their pots of gold in the real estate market, stocks and bonds or inheritance. These statistics suggest where you should invest your money if you ever want genuine financial freedom: invest in yourself!

Each year, thousands of men and women between the ages of thirty-five and fifty-five leave corporate America to pursue their entrepreneurial dreams. Some do it for financial independence, others like the tax advantages, while most are simply looking for job security and the freedom to control their own destiny. But freedom has never been achieved without some inherent risk. The trick is to minimize the risk by following a proven path to success.

Many potential buyers believe the only reason a business is for sale is due to it being in some financial crisis. Realistically, less than twenty percent of the businesses for sale at any given time are drowning in red ink. The majorities are being sold for reasons such as death, divorce, poor health, partnership disputes, and the desire to acquire a larger business, burnout or simply retirement.

One of the keys to any successful negotiation is knowing how the other side thinks and feels. This book is published in two parts to enable buyers and sellers to "tune into" each others' motivations, strategies hopes and fears. By doing so, each can respect what the other is trying to accomplish in the transaction and the two parties can move forward to a win-win consummation.

My motivation for writing this book stems from the thousands of buyers and sellers I interviewed over my thirty-year career and the costly mistakes so many made in the pursuit of their financial and social goals. It is my deepest desire that this book be used as a road map to prevent would-be buyers and sellers from repeating those financially destructive mistakes.

The Chapters dealing with valuing a Business, the Nondisclosure Agreement and the Asset Purchase Agreement have been duplicated in both sections of this book because they are chapters that are vitally important to both the buying and selling process.

CHAPTER ONE:

AN ENTREPRENEURIAL TEST

There is a tremendous interest in entrepreneurial pursuits today. One explanation may lie in the fact, that when corporate America downsizes, as it does during a recession, a key strategy involves the discharge of middle-aged managers at the peak of their earning power. These high-priced executives are generally replaced by younger counterparts hungry for promotion and willing to work long hours for less money in order to achieve that goal. In any event, more and more people are looking to themselves for the answer to future employment. As a result, business sales are on the increase nationwide with the emergence of a new breed of entrepreneur, what I call the "modified risk taker."

My dictionary defines *Entrepreneur* as, "A person who organizes, operates and assumes the risk for a business venture." This definition implies that the "classic entrepreneur" starts a business from scratch - a risky venture at best. However, the "modified risk taker" typically buys an existing business or franchise to bypass most of the start-up risk. In order to further limit risk, would-be entrepreneurs should examine their strengths and weaknesses to see if they are even qualified to consider business ownership, **because not everyone is born to be an entrepreneur.** To see if you possess some of the more vital entrepreneurial traits, I offer the following test…which can also be used as a checklist of the issues to be dealt with prior to starting or acquiring a business.

Yes   No

1. ___ ___ Do you want to own a business bad enough to work long hours with no promise of immediate compensation?

2. ___ ___ Have you ever worked in a business similar to the one you want to buy or start?

3. ___ ___ Have you had any entrepreneurial training (formal or informal)?

4. ___ ___ Are you a self-starter?

5. ___ ___ Do you have the patience and ability to work with and energize people (customers, employees, vendors, landlord, etc.)?

6. ___ ___ Are you a leader?

7. ___ ___ Can you accept total responsibility for a job's success or failure?

8. ___ ___ Are you able to withstand stress?

9. ___ ___ Do you have access to a credible team of experienced and objective advisors?

10. ___ ___ Have you created a business and marketing plan (with a definitive budget) for your acquisition or start-up?

11. ___ ___ Has the plan been critiqued by your team of advisors?

12. ___ ___ Can you make decisions quickly?

13. ___ ___ Do people consider you both trustworthy and creditworthy?

14. ___ ___ Can you stick with a task until it is completed?

15. ___ ___ Are you in good health?

16. ___ ___ Can you access additional capital beyond the initial start-up or acquisition costs (most businesses fail due to a lack of working capital)?

17. ___ ___ Are you prepared to lower your standard of living while your business is getting on its feet?

18. ___ ___ Have you researched the marketability of your product and/or service (lack of research is the second most cited reason for a business's failure)?

19. ___ ___ Have you shopped your competition to determine what your competitive advantages are (if any)?

20. ___ ___ Have you researched the availability of personnel with the skills necessary to staff your business?

21. ___ ___ Do you have a suitable location for your business (for start-ups and new franchises only)?

22. ___ ___ Did you check to see if there were any laws (local, state or federal) that may hamper your ability to do business?

23. ___ ___ If you could make the same (anticipated) amount of money working for another business owner would you still proceed?

24. ___ ___ Do you have the support of your spouse or "significant other?"

25. ___ ___ Are you able to comprehend and create financial statements?

If you answered "yes" to twenty or more questions, you likely possess the attributes to be a "classic entrepreneur" and start a new business. If you answered "yes" to at least 15 questions, you fit the profile of a "modified risk taker" suggesting that you focus on the purchase of an existing business or franchise.

And if you answered "yes" to fewer than 15 questions, in my opinion, you should keep your money in safe investments and retain your day job.

CHAPTER TWO:

HOW TO GO INTO BUSINESS (AN OVERVIEW)

There are four basic ways to go into business:

1) Start one;

2) Purchase an existing business or franchise;

3) Purchase a start-up franchise; or (best of all)

4) Inherit one.

A *start-up* can be the cheapest and most satisfying way to enter the entrepreneurial world, but U.S. Department of Commerce statistics reveal that nearly two-thirds of all start-ups fail in the first three years. This is usually the result of the owners being under-capitalized or foregoing proper market research, e.g. the rise and fall of Albuquerque bagel shops during the 1990s. While demographic studies looked favorable, both franchisors and independents failed to take into account one important fact: most New Mexicans prefer tortillas to bagels. Proper market research would have disclosed that fact. If a would-be entrepreneur wants to eliminate or at least manage risk, a start-up is rarely the answer.

Purchasing an *existing* business or franchise offers the buyer a recognized name, a proven product (or service) **and** a proven location - three of the four most important components of a successful business. The fourth component is a proven financial track record that can be verified with proper due diligence. Armed with the seller's training, consulting and warranties (and often financing), the buyer can assume the ownership role with a large measure of confidence.

Purchasing a *new* franchise offers a lower level of risk than a start-up because you are buying a proven name and product (or service) along with the necessary training and consulting. However, a buyer must still find a suitable location (most often with the franchisor's help) and survive the early growth stages until the business finally makes a profit (usually one to three years). Franchisees must also finance all of the start-up costs through their savings or a bank loan, which may often prove both difficult and expensive. On the plus side, a franchisor's training and on-going assistance help franchisees master such rudiments of business management as marketing, pricing, inventory control, accounts receivable, accounts payable and human resources.

Inheriting a business, while exciting on the surface, may also be a recipe for disaster if the business has serious debt, pending litigation or other money-devouring problems. An Asian friend, I'll call Elena, was a financial partner in a clothing and accessories business that wasn't supposed to involve her on a day-to-day basis. However, when her operating partner decided the business was no longer worth her time or effort (a relatively easy decision for the partner without a monetary investment), my friend was left literally holding the "handbag." Fortunately, she had the patience and persistence to turn the business around into a real money-maker which has allowed her to travel the world looking for fashion ideas.

Regardless of the methodology you choose to become an entrepreneur, one basic fact should be hard-wired into your decision: **ABSENTEE OWNERSHIP DOESN'T WORK!** You have to tend to a business on a daily basis to make it a success. This fact has been proven time and again, so please don't believe you can be the exception.

CHAPTER THREE:

STARTING A BUSINESS

Each year thousands of would-be entrepreneurs take out loans, sign leases and open businesses in search of the elusive American dream: freedom through self employment. Unfortunately, as previously stated, nearly two-thirds fail in their first three years.

What are the winning characteristics of the businesses and owners that are able to survive these sobering statistics? Following is a sampling of the success factors I have observed in my thirty-plus years of business brokerage and consulting.

1. ASSEMBLE A TEAM OF PROFESSIONALS. Consider acquiring the services of an accountant, attorney and commercial real estate agent as you begin your entrepreneurial journey. This decision will be driven by both the size of the start-up you envision as well as your risk tolerance level. An experienced accountant will assist you in developing a realistic budget for the new enterprise while a good business attorney will review any pertinent contracts including a lease. The attorney's and accountant's fees will have to come out of your pocket, but that cost can be minimal when compared to the potential cost of a misguided start-up. A commercial leasing agent will be a valuable asset if you need to negotiate a new lease, and better yet, the agent's fee will likely be paid by the landlord.

2. HAVE A SOUND PLAN. In addition to a great idea, every successful business has a strategic plan that focuses on:

> (a) **The product and/or service**. In order to be successful in today's competitive marketplace, you must differentiate your product or service from that of your competitors. This can be accomplished through upgrading, pricing, post-sale support (i.e. service warranties), availability (real people vs. electronic voices), and target marketing. Remember, all

of your potential customers' needs are currently being satisfied (to a greater or lesser extent) by your competitors. Therefore, you must give them a viable reason to choose you!

(b) **Customer base identification**. The more specific you can be in identifying your targeted client/customer base, the easier it will be to fine tune your marketing efforts. One of the best ways to identify your potential clients is through the use of focus groups, i.e., non-biased and socially diverse people that are paid to evaluate your product or service and provide an honest and practical assessment of both its desirability and viability. This group will focus on the specific gender, age, social and economic characteristics that best define your target market. Important demographic information can also be obtained by visiting www.wikipedia.com and www.census.gov. All would-be entrepreneurs should beware of the pitfalls of relying on the opinions of friends and relatives – they will generally be reluctant to risk their relationships by disclosing their true feelings.

(c) **Marketing and sales**. Once you have identified your potential client base, you can begin to develop a sales and marketing plan to target your advertising to that segment of society. The emergence of social media presents new and exciting avenues through which you can present your message. Sometimes the old standbys, i.e., radio, television, newspaper, magazines, billboards, direct mail, or even door-to-door contacts, can produce the desired results. Small neighborhood businesses can often thrive on just direct mail coupons, parking lot flyers and door hangers, while businesses that require a more diverse customer base may have to turn to mass media. A good advertising agency can assist with these important decisions and design an ad campaign that will bring customers to your business.

Remember, the best overall advertising comes from word-of-mouth referrals that you earn by offering quality products and better than average service. Most importantly, **all businesses need an attractive, easily-accessible and functioning web site.** Money spent on a quality website can produce a tenfold return on investment.

(d) **Employee hiring, training and retention**. Most start-ups begin with the owner performing all the tasks, from cook to cashier, store clerk to stock boy. But as a business grows, it becomes necessary to acquire assistance. The most common mistake many new business owners make is hiring too many employees too quickly. No new hiring should be done until it is absolutely necessary, and even then, it should begin with temps, part-time workers or independent contractors. This will put most of the payroll tax and compliance burden on others, while you retain more of the "cream" that rises to the top.

(e) **Site selection**. Some businesses, such as retail stores and certain service providers, e.g., tax preparers, require more exposure than others, e.g., factories and warehouses. However, generally speaking, the greater the exposure, the higher the rent per square foot (rent for retail and office space can run twenty times more per square foot than manufacturing space). The key is to decide what will work best for your business. Your commercial leasing agent can help you discover the best location for the highest return on your marketing and advertising dollars.

(f) **Interior/exterior design**. The attractiveness of a store front or office may well determine the success or failure of a start-up because no sales are made until a customer enters your place of business. Business facades should be both clean and welcoming. Some businesses use architectural features, e.g., the "golden arches," while others use window displays, flowers, plantings and most importantly, effective signage.

(g) **Signage**. *Cuteness* should always take a back seat to functionality. Some owners get so caught up in developing a funny/*punny* name that they forget the real reason for a sign – to attract customers. ALL signs should clearly state the essence of the business; a gift store sign should contain the word, "gift" or some reasonable synonym. A sign that reads, "Martha's Nook," doesn't convey a reason to stop-in and see Martha's wares or services. My wife, Maggie, who owned an advertising business for two decades, insists that every business name should describe its product or service in order to be an effective advertising vehicle.

(h) **Furniture, fixtures and equipment**. Don't break your budget purchasing new furniture, fixtures or equipment. In most cases, used furniture, fixtures and equipment can be purchased at bargain discounts, especially restaurant equipment and retail fixtures. If an office has to really impress, good, used office furniture from consignment stores will often meet that challenge.

The most important caveat in purchasing used equipment is that it is up-to-date and capable of performing the task for which it was purchased. Several years ago, prior to the digital age, a friend of mine purchased a business that specialized in architectural and engineering blueprints. Unfortunately, he didn't research the industry well enough to discover that the old, bulky ammonia-based systems were being replaced with high-speed digital cameras. He could still do the work, but not with the speed and quality of his more tech-savvy competitors who had acquired state-of-the-art equipment. He unfortunately had to close his business.

(i) **Leasehold interest**. Never purchase commercial real estate when starting a business! It is far more prudent to lease the absolute minimum amount of space to satisfy your current needs. Then, as your business grows, expand into larger quarters. After several months in business, you will have a much better perspective regarding your future space and location requirements, and if you are successful, you will possess the resources to acquire your own piece of real estate in the future.

At the outset, try to commit only to a short-term lease (assuming you can negotiate one with the landlord). A one-year lease with a couple of two-year renewal options will protect your rights to the space, while at the same time protecting your pocketbook in the event your business either isn't successful or must be moved to a bigger/better location in the future.

(j) **Operating Budget**. I have emphasized the budgeting function because this is where the seeds of success or failure are initially sown. If you are unsure how to develop an operating budget, seek help from your accountant or a qualified business consultant before starting on your entrepreneurial journey.

The operating budget is a baseline that allows you to chart the growth (or decline) of your business. Comparing your business's actual performance to its operating budget shows where improvements or changes need to be made. Please note that all budgets should be considered *living organisms* – not cast in stone. New products, services, technologies or unseen exigencies may require some budget modification, but the baseline is always there as a guide. Your best budgeting ally is an accountant who understands your goals and will alert you to budget deviances or aberrations, as they occur, and help you understand their repercussions. Unfortunately, in my thirty-year career, I have encountered only a few such individuals.

3. CASH IS KING. No matter how fine-tuned your budget is, there are always some surprises. I recommend, that once you have determined your annual budget, make sure you have access to a similar amount available as working capital. This enables you to take

advantage of bargains on equipment, try new marketing techniques, hire more employees (as needed), and most importantly, keep your stress level manageable. In order to conserve cash, some entrepreneurs prefer to lease their furniture, fixtures, signs and equipment rather than purchase them outright. Another strategy is to ask your vendors to give you terms for repayment. This is often possible to achieve if your credit is good and your financial statement is solid.

Leasehold improvements can also be pared if you are willing to do some of the work yourself. Landlords will generally allow you to perform such minor tasks as painting, carpeting and other decorative touches. For the big jobs, landlords will often amortize the cost of improvements over the life of the lease and include it in the monthly rent. And never forget, as I alluded to earlier, that thousands of successful businesses were born in garages or spare bedrooms and later moved to storefronts, offices or industrial facilities.

If your start-up involves the manufacturing of a product, consider engaging a contract manufacturer to make it for you. I have a friend with a jewelry manufacturing business who creates high-quality jewelry for designers across the country. Designers send him their sketches and he cranks out the finished products, thus allowing the *entrepreneurs* to concentrate on the design and sales functions and build the manufacturing cost into the price of their products. Best of all, they don't have to deal with the headaches associated with employees, equipment and government-imposed rules and regulations.

4. DO THE RESEARCH. Too many people open restaurants simply because they like to cook and their friends have complimented them on their culinary skills (what friend tells a host the truth when it comes to a bad meal?). Don't guess about the marketability of your product or service. If you really feel you can make a better pizza than Pizza Hut, do as I recommended earlier: hire an advertising agency to arrange a focus group to sample your product. A focus group is paid to be fair and impartial, so leave your sensitivity at the door and listen to the professionals.

It's very important to know and understand your target customer. Just because you covet knick-knacks and collectibles doesn't necessarily mean the world does. In fact, in my experience, gift and collectible shops suffer nearly the same mortality rate as restaurants.

Don't try to compete with Wal-Mart - differentiate! When Wal-Mart came to his small Missouri town, my brother-in-law had the only local shoe store. He saw what the giant retailer carried in shoes (low price and medium quality) and decided to begin offering higher quality and more expensive inventory. It worked!

The famous stripper, Gypsy Rose Lee, once advised, "Ya gotta have a gimmick!" The "gimmick" for a small retail business is SERVICE. "Big box" retailers will usually only deliver large-ticket items but a small entrepreneur can deliver anything. The big guys don't offer their customers soothing refreshments on a hot afternoon - but you can! They generally don't provide post-sale, back-up assistance, but a small, service-oriented business owner will want to because it reinforces a continuing customer relationship.

5. THINK LIKE A CONSUMER. When looking for a business to start, ask yourself (and your friends), what goods and services are not readily available in your market area? Successful entrepreneurs will often do what others either <u>won't do, or can't do</u>. Who asks a plumber how much it's going to cost for an emergency call when the toilet is over-flowing? I chose the business brokerage field because there were few qualified individuals in the marketplace due to the potentially litigious nature of the business and the uncertainty of a straight commission career.

One of the most successful businesses I have encountered is the operation of a "honey wagon," an *affectionate* term for a septic tank pumping business. The owner had two trucks, one of which was driven by a nephew and the other by himself. He <u>netted</u> more than a quarter million dollars a year because he was willing to do what others found repulsive. To him, the business's inherent odor was really the "sweet smell of success!"

6. DON'T BECOME A HOSTAGE. When selecting your new business, make sure you understand all its intricacies so you don't have to rely totally on key employees for your success. It's fine to hire a chef to run your restaurant's kitchen but you should be able to step into that role in the event of a dispute, sickness or other emergency. You don't have to be Wolfgang Puck - you just need to be good enough to fill in during emergencies.

This piece of advice is best exemplified in a real life situation where a "part-time" owner had hired an assistant to operate his business while he pursued other interests. When it came time to sell, the buyer asked for the requisite, on-site training. Because the owner was no longer intimately acquainted with either the business or its customers, he turned to his assistant to provide the training. The assistant, having no future employment prospects following the sale, refused. In order to consummate the sale, the owner had to purchase a new pickup truck for his assistant (at a cost of $20,000) so he would provide the necessary training and consulting for the purchaser of the business. Incidentally, the business sold for only $100,000. The owner had to give up a significant portion of his sale proceeds because he became a *hostage*.

You can also become a hostage to a client or customer. If you depend on a single client or customer for more than fifty percent of your business, you could be in serious trouble if your relationship sours or the client goes out of business.
I once had a business under contract that did seventy percent of its sales with only one governmental agency. While we were preparing for the closing, that agency's budget was cut nearly in half. Upon receiving word of the budget cut, the buyer immediately backed out of the sale despite the seller's offer to reduce the price of the business accordingly. A broad and diversified customer base is a major key to success.

7. NEVER BE TOO PROUD TO ASK FOR ADVICE. Established business owners will often give you the advice you need if you are not a direct competitor. A friend of mine, who owns a very successful painting company, explained that when he started in business, he sought the advice of a well-respected entrepreneur who had hired him

to paint his home. The advice he received over the ensuing months earned him the high standard of living he enjoys today. That advice?

*Pay off your debts as quickly as possible;
*Create a support group for advice;
*Help those around you to succeed; and
*Prepare to give before you can expect to receive.

There are also several helpful organizations such as SCORE (Service Corps of Retired Executives) sponsored by the SBA, local chambers of commerce, and Small Business Development Centers at community colleges. Some colleges even offer personnel assistance to new business owners in the form of student interns who are often eager to work in a business simply for the valuable experience it can afford.

Some enterprising entrepreneurs create their own team of advisors by organizing "leads" or "tips" clubs wherein non-competing business owners or mid-management personnel meet on a weekly basis to exchange information that can help their colleagues realize more sales or gain a competitive advantage. I belonged to such a Tips organization for more than a quarter century and credit a great deal of my success to the information and support I received from that body.

CHAPTER FOUR:

PURCHASING AN EXISTING BUSINESS OR FRANCHISE

The buying process begins with a frank and open assessment of a buyer's resources and acquisition criteria. The purchase of an existing business almost always requires a substantial investment, so it is necessary for buyers to determine the extent of their financial resources. Buyers should also take a hard look at their knowledge bases and reservoirs of experience in order to develop sound acquisition criteria: the type of business to pursue, preferred hours/days of operation, ideal number of employees, required skill sets, price range, location, and market area. This is where teamwork can be invaluable, which may require the services of a business broker, accountant and attorney.

The business broker's job is to introduce you to current acquisition opportunities and advise you in negotiations. The business broker's fee will likely come out of the seller's closing proceeds so it won't affect your cash reserves. An accountant will analyze the financial information provided by the seller and work with the business broker in developing a defensible value to put on the business acquisition. A good business attorney will review any pertinent contracts and assist with the development of a sound purchase agreement. The attorney's and accountant's fees will have to come out of your pocket, but that expense can be minimal when compared to the potential cost of a misguided transaction.

After finding a few interesting business opportunities, it is customary to ask the broker for a professional marketing package on each one. A buyer should expect to sign a Non-disclosure Agreement [see Chapter Five] to assure the seller that all of the proprietary information being provided will be viewed discretely. The marketing package is intended to provide enough data to whet a prospective buyer's appetite for a meeting with the owner and a tour of the business, or to convince the would-be buyer that the business is not a satisfactory fit.

Once the NDA is signed, the broker generally offers the prospective buyer a marketing package that provides detail regarding the business's operations and limited financial information (no tax returns, income statements or balance sheets at this point). If the prospective buyer decides to pursue the acquisition to its next stage, the broker arranges a meeting with the seller wherein the two parties will be able to ask each other pertinent questions. Sometimes sellers prefer the initial meeting to be held in the broker's offices so that total confidentiality is assured. In some cases, the initial meeting takes place at the seller's place of business after business hours. It is the seller's role to decide on the most comfortable scenario.

If a meeting is set, the buyer should bring a list of pertinent questions that weren't covered in the marketing package. There should be no surprise if the business owner refuses to answer some highly proprietary questions dealing with personal finances or the existing customer base. These questions can be answered in the due diligence process following an executed Purchase Agreement [as described in Chapter Eleven].

While touring the business, a buyer needs to determine if the business "fits," much like a dress or new suit of clothes. If it doesn't, the buyer should pass! But if the fit is evident and most acquisition criteria are satisfied, development of a Purchase Agreement with a suitable pricing strategy is in order.

But what if you don't have the requisite down payment? Do you give up on that particular business? Not necessarily! Let me give you an example.

One of the first businesses I sold, as a rookie business broker, was a small escrow company. The seller was asking only $60,000 with $20,000 down...a fairly small deal when compared to million dollar transactions, but one that was nonetheless important to the seller who was seventy years old and ready to retire. Because of the seller's age, he had not concentrated on marketing the business for the past five years, which caused the business to stagnate while at the same time providing an ambitious buyer with a great opportunity.

The first prospective buyer to come on the scene was a young man fresh out of college with a business degree. He had worked in a family-owned escrow company while he attended college and felt it was a good way to enter the business world. Unfortunately, he only had $15,000 as his equity investment. After I cautioned him that he would need some working capital, he made an offer for $60,000 with $10,000 down (leaving $5,000 for his working capital). Like a dutiful broker, I presented the offer to the seller and explained how the buyer, although quite young, had actual experience in the escrow industry and how eager he was to accept the responsibility of adopting the seller's "baby."

The seller was impressed with the prospective buyer's experience and exuberance but felt that, although he really didn't need the extra money, a deal with only $10,000 down was too risky. When I relayed the seller's response to the young would-be entrepreneur, he was understandably disappointed and asked me what he had to do to get the seller to take his offer seriously. I explained to him that all negotiations require a certain balance to make the deal *win-win.*

Because a *typical* sale requires a down payment of thirty to forty percent of the asking price, his offer of less than twenty percent down disturbed the "balance" of the deal. If he wanted the seller to consider his offer, he would have to balance it in some other way that his resources permitted. The strategy we employed was to offer a higher price than the asking price...the thought being, the *risk* needed to be commensurate with the *reward*. We went back to the seller with an offer of $67,000 with $10,000 down...and the seller accepted it. The seller's risk was offset by an anticipated higher return.

So how did it all turn out? That young man's $10,000 investment in a small escrow company grew into a highly successful escrow and mortgage firm with offices in seventeen western communities. **You can't hit a home run unless you find a way to get to the plate!**

If you are considering the purchase of an existing franchise, some of the same rules apply as buying a new franchise [see Chapter Six]. You will want to review a copy of the original Franchise Agreement as well as a copy of the most current Franchise Disclosure Document. The primary difference between the purchase of an existing business and a franchise is the possibility of obtaining seller-financing, which is generally not available in the purchase of a new franchise.

Regardless of the training that a new entrepreneur receives from the franchisor, there is always the need for additional training and assistance on the part of the seller in order to cover all the nuances of doing business is that specific market. Patience and persistence are also necessary virtues.

Back in the 90's I sold a ten-year-old Dairy Queen brazier to a gentleman (whom we'll call Ray) who was intent on moving from California to New Mexico to "start a new life." After three weeks of intensive training at the company's offices in Minneapolis, he returned to New Mexico to consummate his purchase and begin operating the business. Both the seller and his wife were on board for two weeks to assist Ray in getting a "feel" for his new enterprise and to guide him through any surprises. The only surprise came in the form of a hoard of customers craving ice cream and hot dogs. It was, after all, Labor Day weekend - allegedly the second busiest time of the year for ice cream and hot dog consumption - which just happened to occur immediately following the closing.

As the clock neared 5:00 p.m. on Labor Day, Ray took off his apron, handed it to the sellers, and walked out the door and away from his new business and his $45,000 down payment. He simply couldn't handle the stress of trying to service that many demanding customers, despite the sellers' assurances that the Labor Day weekend surge was an aberration. Ray flew back to California the next day and never looked back. The sellers took back the business and we sold it two months later. Patience and persistence!

CHAPTER FIVE:

THE NONDISCLOSURE AGREEMENT

It is the seller's broker's responsibility to market the business and qualify prospective buyers by making sure they have the necessary resources, both financial and intellectual, Once that determination is made, the broker typically requires the potential buyer to sign a non-disclosure agreement (NDA) to ensure the seller's confidentiality through the date of closing. Following is a standard NDA:

In connection with the possible acquisition (the "Proposed Transaction") by you (the "Buyer") of _____(the "Business"), _____ (the "Seller") has furnished you information (the "Proprietary Information") regarding the Business. Buyer acknowledges that the Seller desires to maintain the Confidentiality of the Proprietary Information and agrees not to disclose or permit access to any Proprietary Information, without the prior written consent of Seller, to anyone other than Buyer's legal counsel, accountants, lenders or other agents or advisors to whom disclosure or access is necessary for Buyer to evaluate the Business.

Proprietary Information shall be defined as all information, including the fact that the Business is for sale, in any medium or format, which Buyer receives, either directly or indirectly from the Seller concerning the Business. This definition of Proprietary Information does not include any information that: (a) is readily available and known to the public; (b) is or becomes published on or after the date of disclosure to Buyer; (c) is in the Buyer's possession at the time of disclosure of such information to Buyer by Seller; (d) or is independently developed by the Buyer without reference to or reliance upon information disclosed by the Seller.

In consideration of obtaining said Proprietary Information, Buyer agrees as follows:

1. All of the terms of this Agreement shall remain in effect for Three (3) years from the date hereon.

2. If Buyer decides not to pursue the Proposed Transaction, Buyer will promptly advise Seller of this fact and return to Seller all Proprietary Information furnished to Buyer without retaining copies, summaries, analyses or extracts thereof. Buyer agrees not to use the Proprietary Information to harm the Business by: (a) contacting its customers, employees suppliers or landlords; (b) by lingering or otherwise observing the Business without Seller's consent; (c) or by starting a competing business within the existing market of the Business, if Buyer is not currently doing business within this market. Buyer agrees that it will use the Proprietary Information solely for the purposes of determining whether Buyer would be interested in pursuing a possible acquisition of all or part of the Business.

3. This Agreement shall be construed under and governed by the laws of the State of _____. The venue for any action instituted to enforce any terms of this Agreement shall be in the county in which the Business is located.

This Agreement may be signed in counterparts and faxed and electronic signatures will be considered as originals. If Buyer is a corporation, partnership, limited liability company or any other legal entity other than a sole proprietor, the undersigned executes this Agreement on behalf of Buyer and warrants that he/she is duly authorized to do so. Buyer acknowledges receipt of a fully executed copy of this Agreement.

Agreed to and accepted this ___th day of _____, 20___.

BUYER:

_____   _____
Name (Print)   Signature

Address: _____

_____   _____
Telephone Number   Email Address

CHAPTER SIX:

PURCHASING A NEW FRANCHISE

America has been having a love affair with franchises for more than six decades and it shows no signs of cooling down. The reason behind this seemingly undying romance is the fact that nearly ninety percent of all franchised start-ups are still in existence after eight years. Conversely, as I have previously warned, approximately two-thirds of all regular start-ups fail in their first three years.

The secret to the success of franchises is found in the International Franchise Association (IFA) definition of a franchise: "A continuing relationship in which the owner (the franchisor) of a product, service or method, provides a licensed privilege to do business, along with assistance in organizing, training, managing and merchandizing, in return for some consideration. i.e. payment, from its franchisees." In essence, when you buy a franchise, you buy a learning curve that is the sum-total of the knowledge and experience gained by both the franchisor and its franchisees over the life of the company.

So how do you pick the right franchise opportunity? Here are some guidelines to help you choose the business of your dreams. Most of the information you need can be found in a franchisor's Franchise Disclosure Document (FDD).

1. Make sure the technology or process is understandable. Franchises that require extensive professional or technical expertise can exasperate those who don't possess that particular training or aptitude. That's why there are more fast-food franchises available than accounting franchises. To help ensure your success, pick a franchise that fits your background, pocketbook and educational experience.

2. Review the franchisor's track record. Let sturdier hearts pursue newly emerging franchises while you focus on those that have been in existence for at least five years and have more than twenty-five operating units. Investigate the franchisor's history, paying careful attention to the number of *lawsuits* it has incurred with its franchisees, the overall qualifications of its key personnel, and finally, its financial strength via a thorough review of its most recent income statements and balance sheet (this may be a good time to utilize your accountant's expertise).

3. Understand your commitment. There is no free lunch (not even with a fast-food franchise). You pay for the franchise's name recognition and services with a one-time franchise fee, followed by weekly or monthly royalty payments most often expressed as a percentage of gross sales (typically five to ten percent). Most franchisors also charge a weekly or monthly advertising fee that usually ranges from two to four percent of gross sales. Franchise agreements generally place restrictions on territories, operating hours, products or services, advertising, signage and architecture, and they can last as long as twenty years. To those entrepreneurs who want to play the game fast and loose and on their own terms, a franchise is seldom the answer.

4. Analyze the franchisor's support services. In return for your franchise fee and royalty payments, the franchisor should help you choose a suitable site, design your store or office, purchase equipment and inventory, prepare an ad campaign and even help you find the best financing. Prior to opening for business, you should also receive solid training at the company school or in a successful operating unit. A typical training period can last as long as a month or as little as two weeks. Once the new franchise is up and operating, the franchisor should continue to provide on-going management and marketing assistance as well as improved products or services as they become available. The franchisor's assistance should never be more than a phone call or email away.

5. Call existing franchisees. Each FDD must contain a current list of franchisees, which should be your Fort Knox of information. Contact the ones in the most demographically similar communities, but avoid wasting your time on company-owned stores. Ask the franchisees if they are satisfied with the franchisor's training and support as well as their own profitability. In other words, find out if the franchise is living up to its advance publicity. In my estimation, this is the most important step in the franchise buying process.

6. Get expert advice. Your attorney should look at the franchise agreement before you sign it and your accountant should review a copy of the franchisor's income statement and balance sheet, as well as any other pertinent financial information found in the FDD. The Federal Trade Commission (FTC) limits the financial claims that can be made by the franchisor, so any promises of high profits should be seen as a warning signal.

7. Don't be rushed. The FTC protects "impulse buyers" by mandating a ten-day "cooling-off" period between the time the FDD is received and the signing of the franchise agreement and initial transfer of funds. As a compliance *incentive*, the FTC can assess sizable fines for each violation. In years past, every time a franchise "circus" came to our convention center, I would receive calls from people who unwittingly wrote checks to high-pressure sales personnel. I referred those calls to the FTC. These regulations may change from time to time so verify them by contacting the FTC.

Franchises can be diamonds in the rough for those seeking the safety of an existing business along with the excitement of a start-up. However, like diamonds, the strict rules, weekly or monthly royalties and advertising fees are *forever*. This is the primary reason why many would-be entrepreneurs choose other ways to go into business.

CHAPTER SEVEN:

VALUING A BUSINESS

Over the years I have encountered scores of would-be business buyers and sellers who had one critical shortcoming: they didn't know how to calculate a realistic value for the business they were determined to buy or sell. Unfortunately, in many of these cases they went ahead with the purchase or sale and suffered some tragic consequences. Essentially, their emotions won out over sound logic. A defensible evaluation is the foundation for all the other components of the buying and selling process. It is also the most subjective part of the buying and selling process, requiring both investigative and cognitive skills.

The primary requisite in valuing a business is discovering its true *cash flow*. **I define *cash flow* as: the money that remains unspent after all the <u>necessary</u> expenses of the businesses have been satisfied but before the owner has been compensated and before any debt has been serviced.** As a means of discovery, I question sellers about <u>every</u> expense category to determine if an expense is a true business expense or a *personal* expense, e.g., the owner's auto expenses, travel, or health insurance premiums. I caution sellers that anything deemed "personal" in nature, must be provable. For example, a personal health insurance expense should be backed up with cancelled checks or credit card receipts. I also look specifically for any expenses considered to be non-recurring, such as one-time moving expenses or paid-off equipment leases - all these expenses can be considered part of (added to) the *cash flow*.

As part of my *discovery process*, I also compare every expense category on the seller's tax return to the same expense categories in the previous three years and I require explanations about any major aberrations I find (these same questions will likely be asked by either the buyer or the buyer's accountant during due diligence).

Here's a typical case study from a buyer's perspective. A few years ago I was contacted by a lady who wanted me to "coach" her regarding the acquisition of a retail business in a popular Texas tourist area. The seller was asking $1.2 million for both his business and its real estate. Rachael (not her real name) had already *emotionally* purchased the long-established boutique, but to her credit, she wanted some price verification before making an offer.

In order to evaluate the business, I asked Rachael to get me the following information (the same data I require in most of the evaluations I develop):

1. The last three years of the business's year-end profit and loss statements (P&L's), balance sheets, and tax returns, as well as its most recent P&L and balance sheet;

2. Existing real estate and equipment leases;

3. Existing mortgages on real estate or promissory notes encumbering the *chattel* (an old English term for *tangible assets);*

4. Franchise Disclosure Document (if the business is a franchise);

5. Furniture, fixtures and equipment list (with the seller's best estimate of the current fair market value of the major items);

6. Best estimate of the business's normal inventory level, i.e. the amount of inventory necessary to sustain the operation on a daily basis (at seller's cost);

7. History of the business showing its chain of ownership, any past or pending litigation and the owner's future growth strategies;

8. The business's legal structure: sole proprietor, Sub-chapter S or C corporation, Limited Liability Company (LLC), or

partnership;

9. Employee information (years with the company, duties, wages and benefits);

10. Description of the business facility: location, zoning, size of the building and lot, and any special features (docks, overhead doors, ceiling height, shelving, cranes, paving, fencing, power sources, heating and cooling systems, etc.);

11. Products and/or services offered as well as the normal hours of operation;

12. Client base (list of clients with the percentage of sales each represents, market size, primary competitors, estimated market share and customer demographics);

13. List of all intangible assets such as any patents, trademarks, trade names, websites; email addresses, telephone numbers and copyrights.

Once this information was gathered, I began my "forensic" accounting process. I discussed the property value with the retail specialists in my office. At the heart of the discussion was the question, does being on the National Historic Registry make a property more valuable, and if it did, how much more valuable? To my surprise, the consensus was that being on the National Historic Registry could be a detriment as well as a blessing because of the restrictions that may be placed on the property in order to maintain that designation. In essence, there was no added value for being on the Historic Registry because the financial data already reflected that designation's effects (if any).

I then reviewed the sale prices of properties that had recently sold in other historic districts in her state at the time and found that most of those buildings were sold at multiples between $95.00 and $150.00 per square foot. I asked Rachael to supply me with some comparable sales in her resort area and they showed a similar multiple range of $75.00 to $135.00 per square foot. The subject building was 3,300 square feet in size and situated on a 5,000 square foot lot. If I applied the high end of the multiple range ($135.00 per square foot), the value of the real estate would be nearly $450,000. Using a mid-range multiple of $105.00 per square foot, the value came out to $347,000, which I intended to use in my report. Having established a target range of value for the real estate, I next turned my attention to the value of the retail business.

Small businesses are generally valued at a multiple of 2.0 to 3.0 times cash flow…but what exactly is this mysterious entity called *cash flow*? Apart from my earlier simplistic definition of cash flow, most business appraisers define cash flow as the Earnings of a business Before Interest, Depreciation, Taxes and Amortization (EBIDTA) are expensed. In my compilation of the cash flow, I included all owner compensation, i.e. wages, personal insurance, pension plan and other benefits, because in a small business the owner's compensation can really skew the net profit depending on how well the owner "treats" himself or herself. For example, the more an owner takes out of his or her business in salary and other compensation, the lower the net profit of the business.

Note: The only *interest* expense that should not be included in the cash flow is *floor plan interest*; i.e., the carrying cost that manufacturers charge their dealers for large ticket items such as motor vehicles, campers and major appliances. It is assumed that the purchaser of those types of businesses would continue to incur this expense after the sale.

Like many business owners who own rather than lease their premises, this property owner did not have an *arms-length* lease agreement and therefore was not charging her business any rent. When trying to determine the cash flow of any business, *a premises cost*, i.e., mortgage interest payments or rent, must obviously be included in the operating expenses. If the building's value is estimated to be $347,000 (certainly not more than $450,000), a fair market rent can often be calculated using ten percent of the building's value (a standard percentage commercial real estate agents use in establishing a fair market rent). This method identified a fair market rent of about

$35,000 per year with a top-end of $45,000 (approximately $3,000 to $3,700 per month). The boutique seller agreed to an annual rent figure of $40,000 ($3,333 per month) and was ready to have her attorney prepare a lease based on that amount.

The boutique had a net profit of $39,000, depreciation of $6,000, interest of $14,000, and an owner's compensation package of $55,000, for a total *provable* cash flow of $114,000. When the fair market rent of $40,000 was deducted, the cash flow dropped to $74,000.

Net Profit	$39,000
Depreciation	6,000
Interest	14,000
Compensation	55,000
Unadjusted Cash Flow	$114,000
Less Rent	- 40,000
Adjusted Cash Flow	$74,000

Because the boutique's sales had been slipping over the past three years, I felt a cash flow multiple of 2.4 would be appropriate (this multiple was totally subjective on my part), giving the business a value of about $178,000 (including all of its assets). When the estimated value of the business ($178,000) was added to the estimated value of the real estate ($347,000) the result was a total transaction value of about $525,000 - less than half of the $1.2 million requested by the seller.

Note: This is not meant to demean the seller or the seller's intentions because the seller had never requested a professional evaluation in order to set her asking price.

If Rachael had paid the $1.2 million asking price, which would have required an equity investment (down payment) of more than $250,000, the resulting debt service would have destroyed her financially (assuming a financial entity or the seller would have funded the acquisition). When Rachael reviewed my evaluation, she was understandably extremely disappointed, but nonetheless, happy she hadn't made what could have been the biggest mistake of her life. She followed what has always been my mantra in business: **it is far better to do things right, than fast**!

Contrary to those who cite "rules of thumb" as a basis for valuing a business, I have found that most are not defensible. Those based solely on a multiple of net profit are highly questionable because they can be easily *gerrymandered*, i.e., as mentioned earlier, the net profit of any business can be *adjusted* either upward or downward depending on the amount of the owner's compensation. For example, a business showing a net profit of $50,000 and owner's compensation of $100,000 can be altered to show a net profit of $100,000 if the owner chooses to receive only $50,000 as annual compensation. This is the best example of why, in the evaluation of a small business, all of the owner's compensation must be factored into the cash flow.

The same is true of "rules of thumb" that cite multiples of gross sales. Businesses with identical gross sales can have vastly different cash flows depending on the operating expenses of each business. In fact, I have witnessed two identical fast-food franchises, serving the same product mix and market, that had vastly different cash flows due to the individual franchisee's compensation package.

The acid test for any buyer should be whether or not the cash flow of the business can service (retire) the existing debt, pay the owner a suitable living wage and provide a reasonable return on the owner's initial investment (down payment). **If the business's cash flow does not satisfy those three important requirements, the deal should not be consummated**.

The previous example is a relatively simplistic overview of the evaluation process without showing the actual work that goes into the development of a defensible evaluation. On the following page is a more detailed explanation of the forensic accounting process featuring a fictional profit and loss statement. Much of the remainder of this chapter will focus on the expense categories and numbers shown in the following ABC, Inc. P&L.

ABC, INC. P&L

Gross Sales	$600,000
Cost of Sales	300,000
Gross Profit	300,000
Operating Expenses	
-Advertising	10,000
-Amortization	5,000
-Auto	7,000
-Depreciation	15,000
-Insurance	7,000
-Interest	10,000
-Maintenance	6,000
-Owner's salary	40,000
-Payroll	75,000
-Payroll taxes	15,000
-Professional fees	5,000
-Profit sharing	30,000
-Rent	45,000
-Telephone	8,000
-Travel/entertainment	5,000
-Utilities	7,000
Total Expenses	$290,000
Net Profit	**$14,000**

Following are components of a defensible cash flow as described in the previous pages.

Add Back:	
-Amortization	5,000
-Depreciation	15,000
-Interest	10,000
-Owner's salary	40,000
-Personal leased auto	7,000
-Personal insurance	3,000
-Personal travel	3,000
-Owner's profit sharing	10,000
Total Add-backs:	$93,000
TOTAL CASH FLOW:	**$107,000**

ABC, Inc. has a net profit of $14,000 on sales of $600,000. Included in the annual operating expenses are: amortization ($5,000), depreciation ($15,000), interest ($10,000), owner's salary ($40,000), the owner's leased company car ($7,000), the owner's health insurance premium ($3,000), the owner's personal travel ($3,000), and the owner's portion of profit sharing ($10,000). When added together, the cash flow of this business is a respectable $107,000…which is a far more accurate depiction of its financial performance than just the $14,000 net profit figure. Based on the above data, this business would be worth between $214,000 (using a 2.0 multiple) and $321,000 (using a 3.0 multiple). Applying an average multiple of 2.5, the business is worth about $270,000. In order to more closely define the cash flow multiple, the following factors must be addressed:

1. **Business Age and History** - A well-established business generally commands a higher multiple than one less than three-years-old. This is especially true of a business that enjoys a good reputation and has suffered no damaging litigation nor has any potentially damaging litigation pending.

2. **Revenues** – Obviously growing sales make a business more valuable than one that is just keeping pace with inflation or experiencing shrinking sales.

3. **Employees** - Long-term, skilled and self-motivated employees create a higher multiple, as do key management people who remain on board after the sale. It is also important that employees are being paid a fair wage when compared to the existing labor market.

4. **Equipment** - Up-to-date and well-maintained equipment will often enable a business to command a higher multiple, especially if the equipment will support future growth. Leased equipment doesn't justify a higher multiple (all leased equipment should be identified as such on the equipment list).

5. **Real Estate** - If the business premises are leased, a long-term lease (involving both a fixed term and renewal options), at a fair market rent, is the ideal situation. If the real estate is being sold with the business, it should be priced at or below fair market value to command a higher multiple. A buyer will also want an environmental assessment (phase 1 study) for further peace of mind. Environmental problems can not only lower the multiple but may also be deal killers.

6. **Complexity** - A business that is easy-to-learn is generally more valuable than one requiring technical training. If a special license is required, e.g., general contractor, plumber, electrician, the buyer should be allowed to work under the seller's license until the buyer can qualify for one. The seller should always be willing to provide the training necessary to assure the continued success of the business. Any breech of these standard conditions will lower the multiple.

7. **Customer Base** - A growing and diverse customer base is very important and creates a higher multiple for the business. Conversely, a business that depends on only a few large customers will seldom garner a multiple above 2.5. Other demographic information should also be considered such as the age and income per household within the existing market area.

8. **Magnitude of cash flow** - If the cash flow is less than $50,000, it can't provide much of a living wage for the buyer's family or service much debt, whereas a cash flow above $100,000 is far more desirable and tends to push the multiple higher.

It is important to note that the cash flow multiple can be increased even beyond 3.0 if one or more of the following conditions exist:

a) **The cash flow exceeds $200,000, and even more when it passes $300,000 and $500,000.** This is due to the fact that those higher cash flows can service a great deal more debt and still provide the buyer with an attractive living wage. In these instances, the cash flow multiple can range from 3.0 to as much as 4.0.

b) **There are contracts in place that guarantee a steady revenue stream well into the future.** The best example of this is an insurance agency I sold that had a solid client base, and even if no other new clients were added, it would support the agency if the owner simply serviced the existing accounts. As in the above example, strong contractual relationships can also yield a multiple as high as 4.0.

c) **The business's rate of growth is stellar with no foreseeable slowdown.** Trying to value a "shooting star" is extremely difficult because there is no guarantee that the current rate of growth is sustainable. However, if it appears the business will be able to keep its trajectory for the next couple of years, it may warrant a multiple higher than 3.0.

d) **The company has new products or services in the pipeline that will likely generate additional future cash flow.** Nobody can predict the eventual success or failure of a new product or service, but if they are closely related to the company's proven offerings, the odds are in favor of customer acceptance.

e) **The existing management team will remain in place after the sale.** This most often occurs in the sale of larger businesses that are gobbled up in a merger. The acquiring entity will often pay more in order to maintain the status quo by not having to replace key personnel. It makes for a more seamless transaction and also eliminates a competitor.

The key to <u>every</u> business evaluation is being able to determine the <u>true cash flow</u>. A seller must be able to <u>prove</u> all the cash flow components, i.e., any expense that the seller claims is not business-related or is personal compensation must have a receipt or other validating document supporting the claim. Tax returns are always considered an essential part of this documentation process because they are signed under penalty of perjury.

When reviewing a business's tax returns or P&Ls, it is of paramount importance to realize that there are some accounting issues that can greatly impact the true cash flow calculation:

1. In some instances, such as in the first example where the owner of the business also owns the real estate, the tax return and/or P&L may not show a rental expense. In these situations, it is important to find out what a fair market rent would be for the property and include that expense as a negative add-back in the cash flow calculation.

2. If ma and pa are both working in the business and are included in the owner's or officer's compensation expense, an allowance must be made to cover the cost of replacing one of the two spouses. This approach assumes that most buyers are flying solo and that the subject business has required the production of both spouses. The cost of replacing either ma or pa also becomes a negative add-back.

3. In the case of a Sole Proprietorship, the owner may take his or her salary in the form of a *draw*. This term refers to the owner taking money out of the net profits of the business at certain intervals. A *draw* does not show up as the owner's compensation on the P&L. There is a tendency for an owner to want to include the *draw* in determining cash flow but that could be a huge mistake because a *draw* actually comes out of the net profit of the business and is not a part of the overall P&L expenses. If this is confusing, consider ABC, Inc. If this was a sole Proprietor instead of a Corporation, the owner could choose to take the *owner's salary* as a draw. This would, in essence, eliminate the $40,000 salary as an expense and subsequently increase the net profit by the same amount, bringing it up to $54,000…which would yield the same cash

flow when combined with the "add-backs."

4. Another thing to be aware of is the subject of "Other Income" that sometimes shows up on tax returns. If the Other Income is recurring, such as rebates that are earned <u>every year</u> as a result of sales volume with a specific vendor, it can be counted as part of the *cash flow*. However, as is often the case, if the Other Income is derived from the sale of an asset or some other non-recurring source, it may not be included in the cash flow calculation.

5. Unlike S-Corporations, Limited Liability Companies and Sole Proprietorships, owners of C-Corporations may choose to use a fiscal year other than the typical calendar year interval for preparation of tax returns. This is an important distinction when reviewing tax return information especially during due diligence.

6. Finally, there are situations where the owner's compensation is not listed separately on the P&L or tax return but is included in the overall payroll expense. In these instances, a review of the owner's year-end W-2 form will provide the amount that can be listed as an add-back.

There is a sanity test to employ when trying to decide if a business is fairly priced. As previously referenced on page 24, after a typical down payment (30% to 35%), the business's cash flow should be able to retire the balance of the debt and provide the buyer an adequate living wage. In the previous example (ABC, Inc.), if the buyer put down $90,000 (one-third) on an offer of $270,000, the debt service would be a little more than $2,700 per month $32,000 per year), on a seven year payout, at 7% annual interest (typical sale terms, circa 2014). Given a cash flow of $107,000, after servicing the $32,000 annual debt, the buyer would still have about $75,000 remaining that may be used as personal compensation, to fund an operating account reserve, and provide a return on investment (the down payment). This deal makes good financial sense.

Most cash flow evaluations assume a "turnkey" sale, which includes all of the tangible and intangible assets of the business: inventory, trade name, trademarks, patents, web site(s), telephone numbers, existing beneficial contracts, franchise (if applicable), furniture, fixtures and equipment. Simply stated, all the necessary components that make the business successful are in place at time of closing.

In retail businesses with large inventories, it often happens that the cash flow method of evaluation produces a value less than the asset value of the business. For example, say the cash flow of ABC, Inc. is $107,000 and the company has an inventory (at the company's cost) of about $200,000 along with an estimated value of $75,000 for all its other tangible assets. As previously mentioned, the $107,000 cash flow would yield an estimated value of $270,000 if an average multiple of 2.5 is used. That *cash flow generated value* is less than the estimated asset value, which means some adjustment needs to take place for the evaluation to make sense to a seller.

It is common for retail stores to stock more inventory than is economically feasible or practical, which often forces a costly year-end inventory reduction sale. With a little research, it is possible to determine what a "normal" level of inventory should exist to support a store's sales. In the above example, it was discovered that a normal inventory level of $100,000 was optimal for that type of retail operation. The *cash flow value* of the business, $270,000 (including $100,000 in inventory and $75,000 in tangible assets) now makes sense because it shows about $95,000 in **goodwill** which is the difference between the cash flow generated value of the business and the current value of its assets.

But what happens to the excess $100,000 in inventory? In some cases, the seller allows the buyer to sell the excess inventory on consignment, with the seller reimbursed for the cost of the excess inventory as it is sold. In other instances, the seller holds an inventory reduction sale prior to the consummation of the business sale. I always recommend that the buyer opt for the first scenario which puts the buyer in control of any inventory reduction because a pre-closing inventory liquidation sale can decrease normal customer traffic for several weeks following the closing...which is never a good situation for a new owner.

Here are some frequently asked questions regarding business evaluations:

What role does "potential" play in an evaluation? Sellers often point to *potential* in the evaluation process as rationale for convincing the broker to increase the value. Most experienced brokers explain to sellers, that buyers don't pay extra for the *potential* when acquiring a business because they understand that any *potential* they realize after the sale will be due to their time, hard work and investment. Realistically, a buyer won't purchase a business unless it has at least some potential - but also won't pay extra for any pre-sale potential it exhibits.

Should "projections" be used in the evaluation process? Because all projections are totally subjective, using them to determine the value of future cash flow can be dangerous and possibly lead to a lawsuit if a buyer feels there was any misrepresentation. A seller may feel the projected cash flow is attainable but the buyer may not possess the same work ethic or business acumen, thereby making those projections unattainable for the buyer. If a buyer bases an acquisition decision on a value determined by projected cash flow, there is a danger of overpaying which could result in the buyer's inability to service the debt or receive a living wage.

When evaluating businesses, I choose to rely only upon historic and provable financial data with a focus on the most current three years. Attempting to predict future sales and earnings in today's volatile economy is like trying to pick the winning number on a roulette wheel. Just ask those who lost their shirts in the real estate crash of 2008.

Can "tax issues" affect an evaluation? Prior to consummating a transaction, chattel and tax lien searches are conducted to determine if there are any impediments standing in the way of a closing. If the tax lien search shows there are back taxes due by the business owner, it is paramount that the unpaid taxes be deducted from the cash flow for the years in which the taxes were left unpaid. The assumption is that the purchaser of the business will pay all the state and federal taxes when they come due. In this scenario, the buyer may feel it necessary to re-evaluate the business before the closing can take place.

If the Chattel search shows that money is still owed on some of the tangible assets, the value of those assets must be adjusted downward accordingly and a re-evaluation of the business may be in order.

CHAPTER EIGHT:

THE ABC'S OF FINANCING THE PURCHASE

A. SELLER FINANCING. A typical small business sale is seller-financed, requiring a down payment of thirty to forty percent of the purchase price and a promissory note to the seller for the balance, amortized over five to ten years, at an interest rate of six to seven percent (circa 2014). According to my experience, less than fifty percent of all business sales are bank-financed, usually with SBA-guaranteed bank loans. What makes seller-financed deals more attractive is the fact they are relatively uncomplicated and can be closed in three to four weeks, while SBA/bank transactions can sometimes drag on for months as the paperwork filters through layers of bureaucratic red tape.

There is obviously more risk to the seller in a seller-financed installment sale because the buyer can potentially default on the note payments. A buyer usually offsets this risk by signing personally (personal guarantee) on all of the purchase documents and leases to demonstrate a high level of commitment. This puts the buyer's personal assets at risk in the event of default. In some cases, sellers demand specific collateral for the loan, such as a lien on the buyer's home or some other piece of property, or a financial instrument such as a bank certificate of deposit. However, in most seller-financed transactions, the seller is satisfied with the assets of the business (inventory, furniture, fixtures, equipment and accounts receivable) along with the buyer's personal guarantee, as collateral.

Most buyers prefer a seller-financed transaction because it provides a higher level of comfort to know that the seller has sufficient faith in the ability of both the buyer and the business to justify that risk. Seller-financing also guarantees the buyer a certain level of protection: in the event the seller doesn't perform on post-sale conditions, or the buyer is otherwise financially damaged by the seller's pre-sale actions or omissions, the damages can be offset against the monthly promissory note payments (after the seller has been notified and given ample time to cure those damages).

But what if the business is in a downward spiral and the cash flow isn't sufficient to provide the buyer with a reasonable living wage and retire the debt based on the normal financing conditions described above? Under this scenario the buyer might give the seller a smaller than normal down payment and then amortize the note over ten or fifteen years to keep the payments as low as possible at the outset. A five-year balloon, i.e., a total payoff of the outstanding balance, would help give the seller an incentive to accept an abnormally low down payment and smaller monthly payments. This strategy gives the buyer a chance to grow the business and develop a banking relationship so that the necessary balloon payment can be borrowed from a bank when it comes due in year five.

B. SMALL BUSINESS ADMINISTRATION (SBA)/BANK FINANCING. If a cash sale seems to best fit the situation, there are details that every potential buyer should understand. Banks fundamentally don't lend money to business buyers without a great deal of security. This can be realized through a home equity loan or with an SBA-guaranteed bank loan, which is the more popular of the two methods. Here are the most common questions asked by buyers exploring SBA/Bank financing – please note that all of this information is circa 2014:

> **1. Does the SBA lend money for the purchase of existing businesses or new equipment?** Yes and no. Under its 7-A Program, the SBA will guarantee as much as 85% of loans up to $150,000 and 75% of loans over $150,000. The maximum 7-A loan guarantee amount is $5,000,000.
>
> Under its 504 Program, the SBA directly provides as much as 40% of the total financing while a lender provides 50% and has a first lien on the collateral. 504 loans are used for the purchase or renovation of real estate and equipment, but instead of going through a bank, the loan is made via a Certified Development Company. Like 7-A programs, 504 programs have a maximum loan guarantee of $5 million.

Most banks are reluctant to loan money for the purchase of a business or franchise without an SBA guarantee but commercial real estate loans are usually available through normal banking channels as well the SBA 504 program.

2. Can I borrow 100% of the money I need through an SBA program? No! Some equity participation is generally required on the part of the borrower to defray some of the lender's risk and show genuine commitment. That amount can vary from 10% for low-risk businesses such as medical practices, to as much as 50% for high-risk businesses such as restaurants and gift stores. 10% down is fairly standard for the 504 Program although it can go as high as 20% for special cases. Since the bank is at risk for between 15% and 50% of the loan amount, the borrower's financial statement and credit report will also play a major role in whether or not the bank will make the loan even with the SBA guarantee.

3. Can I obtain financing without putting up the whole down payment? Yes, if the seller is willing to carry back a promissory note for the difference. Sellers are often reluctant to do this because their promissory note is subordinate to the bank's note. This means, that in the event of the buyer's default, the bank has first claim on the borrower's collateral. If there is anything left over, it can go to the seller. Many banks require a seller's note to be in a "standby" position, which means the purchaser can't start paying on the seller's note until the bank deems the business healthy enough to support the two payments. A few banks require some seller-financing to reduce their risk and to keep the seller involved in the success of the business. This, however, is not an SBA requirement.

4. Can I secure a SBA 7-A loan if there is no collateral? Most SBA 7-A loan approvals are based on cash flow (the ability of a business to retire the debt), and not collateral. However, if there is collateral available, the SBA will usually want to place a lien on that collateral.

5. What are the typical terms and conditions for these loans? Most 7-A loans are payable over seven to ten years at a floating interest rate usually about 2.25% to 2.75% over the current prime rate. The 504 program, because it deals with commercial property, allows payments of up to 25 years on the SBA portion of the loan (up to 40% of the entire project cost). SBA loans are never subject to balloon payments. The SBA will also likely require the 7-A borrower to sign a ten-year lease that assures the business will be able to remain at its current, **proven** location during the term of the note.

6. Are there any SBA programs that provide funding for minorities. Generally speaking, SBA lending programs are available to all groups on an equal basis. The SBA's Small Business Resource Guide provides detailed information on all of its programs. Information is also available on its web site, www.sba.gov. Another SBA mandate is to help small businesses obtain government contracts and those programs can be of great assistance to members of minority and socially-disadvantaged groups.

7. What is the preferred lender program (PLP)? Certain banks have chosen to specialize in SBA lending programs and have loan officers specially trained to administer these programs. These banks go through a special certification program, and when successful, are named PLP lenders. I would advise potential borrowers to look to PLP lenders because of their expertise.

8. How else does the SBA help small businesses? In addition to its lending programs, the SBA has cooperative agreements with SCORE (Service Corps of Retired Executives – Counselors to America's Small Businesses), Small Business Development Centers (SBDCs) and Women's Business Centers throughout the country. These SBA Resource Partners can provide valuable advice to both existing entrepreneurs and wannabes.

Note: the SBA information in this chapter was circa 2014 but is fluid. Consult your local SBA office for current lending practices.

C. EARN-OUTS. An "earn-out" allows the buyer to acquire a business at a lower than normal price while offering the seller some upside potential if the business is able to achieve certain future levels of success. Obviously most sellers will refuse this tactic, preferring instead to have a down payment and a secured promissory note representing a fixed price and terms. Most earn-outs only occur when the acquisition involves a failing or static business.

In an earn-out, a target price is established that is usually higher than the original asking price. The actual purchase price is generally far below the target price and the buyer makes a small down payment to offset some of the seller's fears. As the goals are reached, the seller generally receives a fixed percentage of the difference between the initial price paid and the target price, or a percentage of the net profit.

For example, a failing business is offered for sale at a price of $400,000 which reflects the estimated current (used) value of the company's assets but not additional "blue sky" or "goodwill." The buyer offers $600,000 for the business with $50,000 down and the balance to be paid if/when the business reaches pre-determined net income levels over the next four years, e.g. $100,000 per year. If the business doesn't achieve the desired net income level in any given year, no payment is due for that year. In this example the seller has a chance to receive a better than anticipated price for the business if the business succeeds. This creates a genuine motivation for the seller to assist the buyer in hitting the annual net income targets. Obviously, certain expenses, such as the new owner's compensation, must be agreed upon up front so as to guarantee a reasonable expectation of the net profit projections.

In one such transaction, possibly the most *buyer-friendly* deal I have ever experienced, the seller's business was in free-fall. In order to keep the business afloat, its workers employed and the hope of some return on decades of hard work and profitable operations, the seller agreed to an earn-out. In this transaction, the buyer agreed to pay a *target price* of $500,000 ($250,000 higher than the asset value), thereby gaining the seller's attention. The seller received <u>no down payment</u> at closing. Due to the fact the buyer was in the same industry as the seller, there was the distinct possibility that the synergism between the two companies would enable the emerging company to be profitable. Fortunately, this scenario played out to both the buyer's and seller's satisfaction.

Most business brokers represent sellers in a transaction - not buyers, so when confronted with an "earn-out," we invariably advise our sellers not to entertain it. The seller generally receives similar advice from his or her accountant and attorney, but dire circumstances will sometimes dictate abnormally aggressive strategies such as the one described in the above example.

BUT WHAT ABOUT FINANCING THROUGH RELATIVES OR "ANGEL" INVESTORS?

Over my thirty-year business brokerage career I have witnessed scores of would-be entrepreneurs with their hopes pinned on promises from relatives or "angel investors," ranging from a well-to-do uncle to venture capital firms. Remarkably, not one of those financial promises ever panned out...which is why I didn't add this method as section "D" to my financing list.

My experience is, when Uncle Bill is asked to write a check, his altruistic leanings towards his favorite niece or nephew suddenly vanish. If your uncle or any other relative is to be counted upon for an investment, make him or her part of the entire process, from the initial search through due diligence. If an investor helps *write* it (the acquisition plan), the investor will be more inclined to *underwrite* it financially and likely ask little more than a fair return on the investment along with what might be a modest equity participation.

Venture capital firms are another story. If your business plan is compelling enough to attract a venture capital firm, prepare for a grueling battle over control. Because of the inherent risk that venture capital firms incur in each investment, their successes must be significant. Therefore, they will generally insist upon a much higher return on their investment than Uncle Bill. This will be manifest in both the requested interest rate, often in the twelve to eighteen percent range, as well as in their equity (ownership) interest, often more than 51% in order to achieve control.

Regardless of the financing method you employ, the important thing is to get the deal done with the best possible outcome to both parties. As I previously mentioned, you can't hit a home run if you don't get to the plate.

CHAPTER NINE:

NEGOTIATING AN ASSET PURCHASE AGREEMENT

Most buyers are encouraged by their attorneys to purchase <u>only the assets</u> of a closely-held corporation (asset sale) rather than its corporate <u>stock</u> (stock sale) for fear of incurring contingent liabilities that may be lurking in the past and which could return to haunt a new owner. When a person buys the stock of a closely held corporation, he or she is buying the history of that business, which could include a potential lawsuit resulting from an accident or some product failure in previous years.

The only time a stock sale makes sense is when there are valuable contracts in the name of the corporation that may take a great deal of time and effort to transfer to the buyer if done through an asset sale. In this event, the Stock Purchase Agreement should contain *sufficient indemnification and hold harmless* language for the buyer's protection.

A stock sale generally provides better tax treatment to the seller, but because it comes at the expense of the buyer (the buyer must assume the seller's balance sheet with all of its depreciated assets), it usually results in a lower purchase price than with an asset sale. An experienced accountant can provide further rationale and explanation regarding the advantages and disadvantage of a stock sale. However, out of more than 800 transactions that I have overseen, only a handful involved the purchase of corporate stock, so I will not be delving further into that subject in this book.

As previously mentioned, the **Asset Purchase Agreement** should include all of the tangible and intangible assets of the business that make the business run successfully:

    a)   all furniture, fixtures and equipment (in decent working condition) required to operate the business;

b) a normal level of inventory and supplies valued at the seller's cost;

c) a leasehold interest that runs at least as long as the seller's promissory note
(as mentioned in the previous chapter, the SBA will typically require a ten-year lease which can consist of a fixed term plus renewal options);

d) a list of all customers, clients and vendors along with their addresses and other contact information;

e) all company patents, trade names, trademarks, website addresses, telephone numbers, email addresses and business directory ads.

f) any existing franchise agreement, service contracts, equipment leases, Yellow Page contract, website hosting agreement or other beneficial contracts that

g) will allow the buyer to maintain the success of the business.

All of the tangible assets that are to be conveyed in the sale should be defined in an equipment list so that there is no question as to what will be conveyed in the sale and what won't. A complete list of both the tangible and intangible assets will be included in the Bill of Sale and used as collateral to guarantee payment on any promissory note.

Some sellers are reluctant to include the name of their businesses as one of the intangible assets because a business sale can be an emotional roller coaster, i.e., they're selling their "baby." This can be disastrous to a buyer, because the trade name contains much of the "goodwill" associated with the business. Fortunately, most sellers understand this fact and agree to the name transfer. In those instances where the seller and buyer are unable to resolve this conflict, I suggest that the buyer be allowed to use the name through a transition period - often as long as three to five years. For example, if John Doe is selling his business to Amy Smith, during that transition period, the business name, *John Doe Enterprises, Inc.* would remain the same for the first year. After that initial year, the name could segue to *John Doe - Amy Smith Enterprises, Inc.*, which in turn becomes *Doe-Smith, Enterprises, Inc.*, and finally, *Amy Smith, Enterprises, Inc.*

As a buyer, remember that <u>all</u> of the assets, both tangible and intangible, that made the business a success are also important to your success...so any exclusion without a logical explanation, should serve as a red flag.

In situations where the seller of the business also owns the real property (according to my experience less than ten percent of the time), either a lease or purchase of the property should be part of any Purchase Agreement. A lease is often in the best interests of both parties because it preserves the buyer's cash reserves while providing the seller with another source of income in addition to the future appreciation in the property's value. By leasing, the seller also avoids a double tax hit. Buyers can protect their *future* interest in the property by asking the seller for a *first right of refusal* or an *option* to buy the real estate at a later date.

A first right of refusal allows the buyer to be first in line to purchase the property if or when the seller/landlord receives a bona fide offer from an interested third party. It is generally worded in the following manner:

> "In regard to the business property located at _____(address)_____, in the event the owner receives an acceptable offer from a third party for the purchase of the business's premises, the buyer of the business known as (___(business name___) has a *first right of refusal* to meet the terms of that offer, and in doing so, acquire the premises on those same terms and conditions. Buyer will have thirty (30) days, following the owner's notification in writing of the third party offer, to enter into a purchase agreement for said property. In the event buyer does not execute a purchase agreement within the thirty-day period, owner shall have the right to sell the property to the third party."

An option to purchase is different from a *first right of refusal* because it is executed at the same time as the buyer purchases the business and it stipulates a fixed future price and terms at that time, or at the very least, a formula whereby the business buyer and property owner can determine the future value of the property. One popular method is for
each party to hire an appraiser and then attempt to have them achieve a meeting of the minds. If that doesn't work, a third appraiser, acceptable to both of the other appraisers, is then hired as a mediator. An option to purchase is typically worded as follows:

> "Seller hereby grants to buyer an option to purchase the real estate located at (__address__) and identified as (_name of business_), on the following terms and conditions (__price and terms or formula__) until (__termination date__). In the event buyer does not purchase the subject real estate within that time period, seller will no longer be bound by the option to purchase and may sell the real estate to a third party."

Once the buyer completes due diligence, the Purchase Agreement is given to an escrow attorney who transforms the abbreviated Purchase Agreement into the final, multi-page closing documents that encompass all the legalese necessary to make the buyer and seller feel comfortable, while allowing their respective attorneys to believe they have protected their clients to the best of their abilities.

CHAPTER TEN:
UNDERSTANDING THE ASSET PURCHASE AGREEMENT

In addition to enumerating both the tangible and intangible assets being purchased, the Purchase Agreement should contain all of the terms and conditions that are necessary for the transaction to be fair and balanced. That doesn't guarantee that all of the buyer's desires will be realized, but it's a good platform from which to launch the attempted acquisition. It's important to note the sale price may not be the most important factor in negotiations - sometimes it is preempted by such factors as the size of the requested down payment or monthly payments, length of training and consulting, or the ability to obtain a suitable new lease or lease assignment.

Purchase Agreements generally contain a list of **contingencies**, i.e., issues that must be satisfied <u>before</u> closing, such as: (a) an inspection of books, records and equipment (due diligence); (b) acquisition of financing if the transaction is not being seller-financed; (c) negotiation of a suitable new lease or lease assignment; or (d) obtaining the approval of a franchisor or key vendor. All contingencies require a deadline for completion so they don't drag on indefinitely. In the event any contingency is not satisfied within the stated time frame, the transaction may be terminated and the buyer's earnest money refunded.

Purchase Agreements also include **conditions**, i.e., items that <u>follow</u> the closing, such as: (a) adequate free training (the time frame depends on the complexity of the business and the relative experience of the buyer); (b) free consulting (primarily by telephone) that follows the training period; and (c) a non-compete agreement (typically for five years and limited to the business's existing market area).

The following pages contain an outline of a standard Purchase Agreement (Offer for Purchase) that has been reviewed by several lawyers who have found it useful as the initial purchase document. Unlike a Letter of Intent, the Purchase Agreement is a binding contract that, when all the contingencies are satisfied, becomes the governing document.

Letters of Intent, on the other hand, are never binding and only touch on the pertinent issues that are routinely addressed in a Purchase Agreement. For that reason, I strongly discouraged the use of Letters of Intent.

Once the purchaser has completed due diligence and approved and accepted the reviewed information, the earnest money deposit usually becomes non-refundable should the buyer decide to back out of the deal. This is why the process of due diligence, as defined in Chapter 12, is so important and should never be rushed.

Following are some general guidelines regarding specific terms and conditions to be found in the Purchase Agreement (Chapter 11) to help you fill in the blanks.

PARAGRAPH #1 - DEPOSIT AND LIST OF ASSETS. Normally two percent to five percent of the total purchase price is a suitable earnest money deposit. The "ownership" of the business refers to the <u>legal</u> entity, <u>not the individual owner</u>, i.e., the corporation, partnership or limited liability company. The only time an individual's name appears on this line is when the business is a sole proprietorship.

As previously stated, the list of assets to be conveyed is vitally important because it specifically defines what the buyer is actually purchasing. All of the items listed in this paragraph are considered to be essential to the continuing operation of the business. In some cases, the seller may have a sentimental attachment to the business's name and ask that it not be included in the sale. The ONLY time this should be allowed is when the business is damaged by the name due to negative goodwill. Otherwise the name is an essential asset to the business's ongoing viability.

Some business web sites are owned by the host company that constructed the web site and are only leased to the business. That is why the conveyance language states that only the seller's ownership interest in the web site is being transferred.

If the business has equipment leases, they must be conveyed through lease assignments that become effective upon closing. Generally a phone call to the leasing company will generate the necessary paperwork for these assignments. It may be necessary to add other items to this paragraph, based on the final negotiations, such as the word, "franchise," if an existing franchise is being purchased.

PARAGRAPH #2 - TERMS. This contract assumes that the deal will be financed by the seller, which is the most prevalent small business acquisition scenario. However, in the event of a *cash* transaction, 2(a) would be changed to read, " Deposit on the date of this agreement included in the total Purchase Price," 2(b) would also be changed to read, " Balance of Purchase Price to be deposited in cash or certified funds, with Escrow Agent at closing," and 2(c) and 2(d) would be eliminated.

Returning to the seller-financed scenario, the purchase price should be expressed in writing as well as numerically. However, the down payment, number of years to retire the note, and interest rate can all be listed numerically. On line 2(a) the earnest money deposit should be repeated because it will be part of the down payment expressed on lines 2(b) and 2(c). Lines 2(a) and 2(b) should add up to the total down payment listed on line 2(c). Line 2(d) reflects the balance of the Purchase Price to be financed by the seller after the earnest money and down payment are deducted. This paragraph also defines the terms of payment, i.e., the monthly payment amount, number of payments due and interest rate. Today (circa 2014), the typical term is seven years and the going interest rate is around six percent. You can calculate the monthly payment by going on-line to one of several websites such as www.bankrate.com.

PARAGRAPH #3 - ESCROW/CLOSING. Seller-financed deals usually take no more than a month to close, but Franchises and SBA/Bank transactions may take more than two months (most franchises require the buyer to undergo extensive training prior to closing; SBA-financed sales must wade through a quagmire of red tap before they are funded). The neutral Escrow Attorney will usually need about a week to prepare the closing documents and order both the chattel and tax lien searches to determine if there are any liens or encumbrances that might interfere with the conveyance of the assets and block the closing.

The escrow attorney can be any attorney willing to serve as a "neutral" party in the transaction, preparing documents that are both fair and protective of both parties. The escrow attorneys I have used typically charged between $1,000.00 and $2,000.00 to prepare the final closing documents. To ensure the closing attorney's neutrality, his fees are split between buyer and seller.

PARAGRAPH #4 - INVENTORY. This paragraph is only used when a buyer is purchasing a business that has either a raw material or finished goods inventory - usually retail, wholesale or manufacturing businesses. The amount of inventory to be conveyed in a sale should be at a normal operating level, at the seller's cost, so the transaction is essentially turnkey, meaning all the components are in place to enable the buyer to begin operating the business immediately (and effectively) upon possession. The purchase price and promissory note are adjusted accordingly if the Inventory shown in the Purchase Agreement differs from the actual inventory count taken just prior to closing.

In the event of a *cash* sale only the purchase price will be adjusted for any inventory variance.

It is customary for the Inventory to be counted by the buyer and seller. If an inventory counting service is used, the fee should be shared equally by the two parties and language to that effect should be inserted into Paragraph #4.

PARAGRAPH #5 - SELLER'S WARRANTIES. This paragraph outlines the protections afforded the buyer and Paragraph 5(c) allows the buyer to offset any damages incurred from a breach of these warranties against the seller's promissory note. For example, if a claim is made against the business as a result of some action (or inaction) taken by the seller prior to the closing, the buyer has the ability to contact the seller and ask for resolution, and if the obligation is not resolved within a reasonable period of time, to deduct the amount of the claim from future promissory note payments until the claim is satisfied.

The concept of "offset" is the buyer's ultimate protection in a business sale transaction. The seller's ultimate protection is the buyer's personal guarantee on any promissory note or lease.

In the event of a *cash* sale, the offset language in 5(c) is changed to reflect the use of an escrow account rather than a promissory note. It is both fair and advisable for the buyer to ask that a portion of the seller's closing proceeds (usually 10% to 15%) be placed in an escrow account and that escrow instructions be incorporated in the closing documents allowing the buyer to offset any damages incurred after closing as expressed in the above paragraph.

PARAGRAPH #6 - SCOPE OF AGREEMENT. This paragraph simply means that any changes to the Purchase Agreement must be in writing and agreed to by both parties, otherwise the Agreement stands as written.

PARAGRAPH #7 - CLIENT/VENDOR LISTS. This paragraph conveys to the buyer all customer and vendor lists - two of the most important assets in a successful business.

PARAGRAPH #8 - LEASE. It's important that the lease term be at least as long as the financing commitment. This can be accomplished with a fixed-term lease, e.g., seven years, or a lease with options, e.g., an initial term of three years with two, two-year renewal options. In the event of SBA/bank financing, a ten-year lease may be required. This can also be realized in segments, e.g., a base term of four years with two, three-year renewal options (or any other combination of fixed-term and renewals adding up to ten years that is acceptable to both landlord and tenant).

If the seller was initially required to provide a lease deposit, it will be the buyer's responsibility to replace that deposit at the closing. In most cases, a new lease or lease assignment [Chapter 15, page 63] will be in place at the time of closing, BUT, the wording expressly states that the lease is null and void if the closing does not occur.

In the event the buyer of the business is also purchasing and not leasing the real estate, this paragraph should be changed to reflect that fact. The following language may then be substituted: *"Seller owns the premises where the Business is conducted and Purchaser is not obligated to close on the sale of the business unless the Seller and Purchaser, prior to closing on the sale of the business, have negotiated a suitable purchase agreement for the subject real estate, which closing shall immediately coincide with the closing of the business sale. If the Purchaser and Seller are unable to negotiate a suitable purchase agreement for the subject real estate, this Offer to Purchase will be terminated and the Purchaser's Deposit will be refunded."*

PARAGRAPH #9 - DISPUTE RESOLUTION. The purpose of this paragraph is to help buyers and sellers resolve any disputes through arbitration rather than having to resort to litigation. However, in the event the matter must be settled in court, this paragraph mandates that the loser will pay the winner's attorney's fees and court costs. This provision is designed to discourage frivolous or unnecessary lawsuits.

PARAGRAPH #10 - EXAMINATION OF BOOKS, RECORDS AND ASSETS. This paragraph defines the *due diligence* period during which a buyer may inspect or review <u>anything</u> he or she feels is pertinent to a comfortable and successful consummation of the purchase. Any refusal by the seller to provide the requested information should be seen as a "red flag" and possibly warrant the buyer's termination of the Purchaser Agreement. The usual time frame for due diligence is two to three weeks. This is one of the most critical periods in the business buying process and the buyer is encouraged to ask for an accountant's assistance.

Once the buyer is satisfied that the business's financial records and assets are as represented by the seller, the buyer will be asked to sign a release of this contingency, thereby making the earnest money non-refundable. At that time, the Purchase Agreement is usually turned over to the closing attorney for preparation of final closing documents.

The language for the removal of the *due diligence* contingency is as follows:

CONTINGENCY REMOVAL FORM

TO WHOM IT MAY CONCERN: I/We, the undersigned Buyer(s) of that certain business known as:

    Business Name: _____
    Located at: _____
    City, State, Zip:_____
hereby remove the following contingency on that certain Offer to Purchase dated _____, 20__ which reads:

Paragraph 10. EXAMINATION OF BOOKS RECORDS AND ASSETS. "Purchaser shall have _____ (_) days after Seller's acceptance of this Offer to Purchase, and after gaining access to the following items, to complete an examination of the furniture, fixtures, equipment, books, records, workers' compensation history, contracts and such other information deemed pertinent to the Seller's business by Purchaser, and Purchaser will rely solely on that personal inspection in making this Offer to Purchase. In the event this Contingency is not removed in writing by the end of the examination period, this Offer to Purchase shall be terminated and the Purchaser's Deposit shall be refunded. "

It is understood by the parties hereto, that upon the execution of this release of contingency, Purchaser's earnest money shall be deemed non-refundable.

All other terms and conditions of the Offer to Purchase will remain unchanged. Receipt of a copy of this Contingency Removal Form is hereby acknowledged.

_____   _____
    Purchaser   Purchaser

_____   _____
    Date   Date

PARAGRAPH #11 - TRAINING AND CONSULTING. A typical training period for a non-technical business is one to two months, followed by a three to six-month consulting period. If the business is especially complicated or its success is due to close personal relationships between the seller and the customer base, a longer transition period will likely be required.

In some extreme cases, such as the sale of a professional practice (accounting, medical, dental, etc.), it is not unusual for the buyer to insist on as much as a year of on-site consulting. It is normal for the buyer to expect the seller to spend at least four to six hours, per normal work day, in the business during the initial training period. Such short-term training and consulting are typically free. If the sale requires some longer-term involvement on the part of the seller, a compensation package can usually be negotiated.

In the sale of an existing franchise, the franchisor will require the buyer to attend the franchisor's training school prior to closing, which can last as little as a week or as long as two months, depending on the complexity of the franchise. This additional time frame must be addressed when choosing a closing date (see Paragraph #3).

PARAGRAPH #12 - ASSIGNMENT OF CONTRACTS. The buyer has the right to ask the seller for copies of all contracts relating to the business that the buyer feels will help ensure the business's future success. This may include equipment leases, service contracts, the yellow page contract, vendor agreements, website hosting contracts, etc. The seller should be asked for a complete list of any such contracts, leases or agreements during due diligence.

PARAGRAPH #13 - COVENANT NOT TO COMPETE. <u>Every</u> business sale should include a covenant not to compete that prevents the seller from starting or purchasing a similar business within the current business's market area. In the event the seller has multiple competing businesses, the non-compete agreement must be carefully structured to protect the buyer from further infringement in the subject business's market area.

A non-compete agreement must contain three components to be enforceable: time, distance and compensation. The typical time frame for a non-compete agreement is five years and it should cover the market area currently being served by the business. This can be expressed in terms of the general area surrounding the business, e.g. within a two-mile radius of the business, or a geographic delineation, e.g., the county, city or state in which the business operates. The compensation is generally a part of the purchase price and shown in the Allocations in paragraph #15.

If the non-compete agreement is overstate: any extreme or broad interpretation, e.g. distance (the entire state for a neighborhood restaurant), or time (ten or more years), it may render the non-compete agreement unenforceable. It is important to note that regardless of the amount of money that is allocated to the non-compete agreement in paragraph #15, it does not the limit the damages that a court may award the buyer in the event of a breach of the non-compete by the seller.

PARAGRAPH #14 - NAME CHANGE. In cases where the name of the business is similar to that of the legal entity, e.g., Acme Window, Inc. doing business as Acme Window, the seller needs to change the name of the legal entity immediately after closing so there is no confusion on the part of the public, the government or financial institutions.

PARAGRAPH #15 - ALLOCATIONS. Buyers and Sellers may wish to talk to their CPA's about this paragraph, as both parties must agree on the Allocations for tax purposes. Most buyers use the Furniture, Fixtures, Equipment and Inventory figures from the marketing brochure or package for those two figures. The Non-compete portion shouldn't be much more than twenty percent of the purchase price in order to satisfy the IRS, and the Goodwill usually covers the balance required so the Allocations add up to the total purchase price. Sellers like to allocate as much of the purchase price as possible to *goodwill* because it is treated as capital gains, resulting in a lesser tax than that attached to ordinary income. Buyers, on the other hand, prefer to allocate as much as possible to furniture, fixtures and equipment, because hard assets can be depreciated over time and provide a tax write-off.

PARAGRAPH #16 - CASH/ACCOUNTS RECEIVABLE/ACCOUNTS PAYABLE. In most business sales, the seller retains the existing cash and accounts receivable and retires any accounts payable and other debts that exist at time of closing. However, in some cases, where the buyer is willing to reimburse the seller for the cash and accounts receivable and assume the accounts payable and other debt to maintain the existing cash flow, this paragraph must be rewritten to reflect those changes. In these situations, the buyer and seller should agree on a baseline figure for both the accounts receivable and accounts payable and then adjust the seller's promissory note at a later date (usually after ninety days) for any difference between the agreed-upon baseline amount and what was actually collected as accounts receivable or paid as accounts payable.

For example, if at the time of closing the Cash and Accounts Receivable total $50,000 and the Accounts Payable and other debt total $40,000, the Buyer would have to pay the seller the $10,000.00 difference at closing. After ninety days, if the buyer was able to collect all but $5,000.00 of the outstanding Accounts Receivable, the $5,000 difference would be deducted from the seller's promissory note. The seller would then be allowed to pursue the delinquent payments through legal channels.

PARAGRAPH #17 - FINANCING. If institutional financing is required in lieu of a seller-held note, the buyer should allow about three to five weeks for a bank to make its loan commitment. As previously stated, SBA/bank financing can take as long as two months to secure, so the closing date should reflect this added time. If the sale is to be seller-financed, this paragraph should be expunged.

PARAGRAPH #18 - ACCEPTANCE OF OFFER. A typical response period is three to five days from the time the broker submits the buyer's offer to the seller. Additional time may be requested if the seller wishes to have the offer reviewed by an attorney or some other entity.

CHAPTER ELEVEN:

THE ASSET PURCHASE AGREEMENT

1. DEPOSIT. Received from_____, or Assigns (herein, "PURCHASER"), on _____, 20___, the sum of ____ _____ Thousand and no/100 Dollars ($_____.00) in the form of a check as an earnest money deposit (herein, "Deposit") on the purchase price of all furniture, fixtures, equipment, leases, goodwill, inventory, trademarks, telephone numbers, the Yellow Pages advertising contract through its current term, trade names, web site (to the extent of Seller's ownership interest), client lists and other tangible and intangible assets of that Business

known as: _____ (herein, "Business"),

owned by: _____ (herein, "Seller"), and

located at: _____

PURCHASER AND SELLER do hereby, jointly and severally, direct and authorize _____, (herein, "Escrow Agent") to deposit amounts of earnest money, and hold same in Escrow Agent's trust account.

2. TERMS. The total Purchase Price of _____Thousand and No/100 dollars ($_____.00) shall be paid as follows:

a. $_____.00 Deposit on the date of this agreement included in down payment.

b. $_____.00 Balance of down payment to be deposited in cash or certified funds, with Escrow Agent at closing.

c. $_____.00 Total Down Payment.

d. $_____.00 Balance of Purchase Price to be paid to the Seller pursuant to a Secured Promissory Note ("Seller's Note") in said amount, payable at $_____.00, or more per month for __ months, with interest thereon at __% per annum, together with a security agreement and a financing statement as provided by the Uniform Commercial Code of the State of _____ which shall be filed with the appropriate State Agency. **Said Promissory Note shall include the Purchaser's personal guarantee.**

$_____.00 TOTAL PURCHASE PRICE

3. ESCROW/CLOSING. For the purpose of completing this transaction, escrow shall be opened at the office of Escrow Agent and closing shall take place on or before 3:00 P.M. on _____, 20__. Escrow Agent is hereby authorized to prepare the necessary closing documents for the consummation of this transaction. All closing costs, including Escrow Agent's fees, shall be paid equally by Seller and Purchaser.

4. INVENTORY. The Purchase Price includes an allocation of $_____.00 for Inventory valued at Seller's cost. If actual Inventory is determined to be more or less than that amount, the Purchase Price and Seller's Note will be adjusted accordingly. Inventory is to be counted and priced by Seller and Purchaser.

5. SELLER'S WARRANTIES. Seller hereby warrants that:

    a. At the time of physical possession by Purchaser, all of the Business equipment will be in good working order and will pass all inspections necessary to conduct such business. Possession shall take place at closing.

    b. It has good, clear, recorded, and marketable title to all of the Business assets being conveyed in this transaction as mentioned above.

    c. All representations made to Purchaser by Seller regarding this transaction are true and accurate to the best of Seller's knowledge, and

Seller grants Purchaser the right to set off any damages suffered by Purchaser, as a result of any breach of any of Seller's warranties or representations, against Seller's Note.

    d. To the best of Seller's knowledge, the above Business, its assets, and its leasehold are in full compliance with all federal, state, and municipal laws, rules, ordinances, regulations, and requirements, and there has been no spill or discharge of any hazardous substance or waste on those premises.

6. SCOPE OF AGREEMENT. This Agreement, and any other exhibits and addenda attached hereto and any documents subsequently signed by the parties, constitute the entire Agreement; there are no oral agreements, understandings or representations being relied upon by the parties; and all prior negotiations, agreements and understandings, written or verbal, are superseded by this Agreement. Any modifications must be in writing and signed by all the parties to this Agreement. Should there be any conflict between the provisions of this Agreement and any escrow instructions executed pursuant hereto, the provisions of the final Closing Documents shall control.

7. CLIENT/VENDOR LISTS. Seller agrees to deliver all lists of Clients and Vendors to Purchaser at time of closing.

8. LEASE. Seller leases the premises where the Business is conducted and the Purchaser is not obligated to close unless the Seller delivers, at closing, a suitable new Lease, an assignment of the existing lease, or a sublease, with respect to the Business premises having a term of not less than _____ (__) months at a base rent of $_____.00 per month. Purchaser will have five (5) days after receipt of a copy of the new Lease, Assignment of existing Lease or Sublease to reject it, or it will be deemed approved. If Purchaser rejects, or Seller is unable to deliver a suitable new Lease, an Assignment of the existing Lease or a Sublease, this Offer to Purchase will be terminated and the Purchaser's Deposit will be refunded.

9. DISPUTE RESOLUTION. If a dispute arises out of or relates to this Agreement or its breach, the Seller and Purchaser shall endeavor to settle the dispute through direct discussions. If the dispute cannot

be settled through direct discussions, Seller and Purchaser shall endeavor to settle the dispute by arbitration before recourse to litigation. The location of the arbitration shall be in _____ or such other location as agreed to by Seller and Purchaser. Seller and Purchaser further agree, that in the event any litigation is instituted to enforce or interpret any of the provisions of this Agreement or for any other reasons, the prevailing party shall be entitled to recover from the other its reasonable attorney's fees and court costs, including appeals, as determined by the Court in such action or suit.

10. EXAMINATION OF BOOKS, RECORDS AND ASSETS. Purchaser shall have _____ (__) days after Seller's acceptance of this Offer to Purchase, and after gaining access to the following items, to complete an examination of the furniture, fixtures, equipment, books, records, workers' compensation history, contracts, and such other information deemed pertinent to Seller's business by Purchaser, and Purchaser will rely solely on that personal inspection in making this Offer to Purchase. In the event this contingency is not removed in writing by the end of the examination period, this Offer to Purchase shall be terminated and Purchaser's Deposit shall be refunded. [See language to remove this contingency on page 43].

11. TRAINING AND CONSULTING. Seller agrees to train Purchaser in the operation of the Business, at no additional charge to purchaser, for a period of _____ (__) weeks from closing. Training shall take place at the Business location and shall consist of a minimum of _____ (__) hours per day. No training will be required of Seller on weekends. Following the initial training period, Seller will act as consultant to Purchaser for a period of _____ (__) additional months - consulting to be performed by Seller primarily by telephone.

12. ASSIGNMENT OF CONTRACT(S). Seller hereby agrees to assign all rights to the Purchaser, in any contracts benefiting Purchaser, including but not limited to those dealing with: Yellow Pages advertising, web site maintenance, equipment maintenance and service, vendor discounts, etc., that exist at time of closing.

13. COVENANT NOT TO COMPETE. Seller hereby agrees not to compete with Purchaser, either directly or indirectly in the operation of the above Business, for a period of _____ (__) years from date of closing, and in an area defined as _____.

14. NAME CHANGE. In the event Seller's corporate name is the same or very similar to the name of the business being conveyed, Seller hereby agrees to either change the name of its corporation, or dissolve the corporation, no later than thirty (30) days following closing.

15. ALLOCATIONS. Seller and Purchaser agree that the Purchase Price shall be allocated as follows:
    a) Furniture, Fixtures & Equipment $_____.00
    b) Inventory   _____.00
    c) Non-compete Agreement   _____.00
    d) Goodwill, Client Lists, etc.   _____.00

        Total: $

16. CASH/ACCOUNTS RECEIVABLE/ACCOUNTS PAYABLE. At closing, Seller shall retain all Cash on Hand and Accounts Receivable, and further agrees to pay all Accounts Payable and other debts or encumbrances against the above Business unless otherwise specified in this Agreement.

17. FINANCING. This sale is contingent upon Purchaser being able to secure suitable financing from a bona fide lending institution within _____ days from the date of this Offer to Purchase. If Purchaser is unable to obtain a financing commitment within this period of time, this Offer to Purchase will be terminated and Purchaser's Deposit will be refunded.

18. ACCEPTANCE OF OFFER. When signed by the Purchaser, this deposit receipt is an Offer to Purchase the above business on terms stated, and should Seller fail to accept this offer by signature hereon prior to 6:00 p.m., _____, 20__, this Offer to Purchase will be terminated and Purchaser's Deposit will be refunded

****

PURCHASER and SELLER individually acknowledge the receipt of a copy of this Agreement. This is a legally binding document. Please read it carefully. If you do not understand it, consult an attorney.

****

PURCHASER hereby agrees to buy the Business on the terms set forth above.

Dated: _____, 20___   At: _____AM _____PM

Purchaser: _____

Address: _____
_____

Signature(s): _____

SELLER hereby agrees to sell the Business on the terms set forth above.

Dated: _____, 20___   At: _____AM _____PM

Seller: _____

Address: _____
_____

Signature: _____

****

DISCLAIMER: This Offer for Purchase and Sale of Assets, Earnest Money Receipt and Agreement (Purchase Agreement) has been in use for more than thirty years in the author's home state of New Mexico and has undergone several modifications and updates by New Mexico attorneys and accountants. The author does not guarantee either its legality or functionality in any other venue. However, in the author's best judgment, all of the warranties, representations, conditions and contingencies that are expressed in this Purchase Agreement should be included, in some manner, in every purchase agreement regardless of the venue or jurisdiction.

As is the case with all legal documents, this Purchase Agreement should be reviewed by an attorney knowledgeable in contract and business law.

****

CHAPTER TWELVE:

THE ART OF DUE DILIGENCE

Thinking about buying or investing in a business? How can you tell if it really is a viable and relatively safe business with long-term income and cash flow potential? The answer is in performing proper due diligence - legalese meaning, *turn over enough rocks to make sure there are no scorpions in the flower garden.*

Many would-be entrepreneurs and/or investors think that reviewing a company's balance sheets and income statements constitutes due diligence. But that should only be the start of a more deliberate process. Here are some other items that warrant close inspection before you sign the final closing documents. If due diligence doesn't turn up any negative vibes, you can proceed to the closing table with confidence. However, if you uncover reasons to believe the business isn't as advertised, you have one of three choices to make: (a) move ahead with the deal; (b) terminate the transaction and have your earnest money deposit returned; or (c) amend the deal to your satisfaction.

    1. Client List. Find out if most of the company's business is done with just a few entities or individuals or if there is a diversified and extensive customer base. If there is a limited clientele, you may want to meet with some of the largest clients as a part of the due diligence in order to determine if they will remain loyal to the business after the sale. Because of the seller's need for confidentiality, any such contacts would occur only after all other due diligence has been performed, and only then under the seller's scrutiny and just prior to the closing of the sale.

    2. Key Employees. If you are looking at a company that relies on key people to perform its services or processes and you do not possess the necessary skills to run the company in their absence, protect yourself! A confidential meeting with key employees can help you determine if you will be able to retain their loyalty and cooperation after the closing. My experience dictates that most employees will wish to remain with the business after the sale because a change of ownership is not nearly as traumatic as a change in employment.

One of a buyer's biggest fears is that all the employees will walk out the door after the closing due to some unrealistic loyalty to the former owner and fear of the "unknown newcomer." Contrarily, many employees fear that the buyer will replace them with family members, personal friends or acquaintances. In my thirty-year career I have never known these fears to become reality because one of the most important assets of the business is its tried and tested employees.

3. **Books and Records**. This is where the "rubber meets the road." Tax returns are signed under penalty of perjury and should always be used to verify income statements, so ask for copies of both for the last three years. The _only_ exception is when the subject business is a subsidiary of a larger corporation and does not file a separate tax return. In this situation, the buyer has no other choice than to rely on only the income statements…which makes the seller's representation and warranties in the purchase agreement even more important.

Beware the seller's statement, "The books don't show all of the money I take from the business." When I hear this disclosure, I tell sellers, "I can only help you sell what you can _prove_." Buyers should retain these words as their mantra.

Other records to review include: a current balance sheet showing accounts receivable and accounts payable; all property and/or equipment leases; pertinent contracts; warranties; patents, copyrights and trademarks (if any), and copies of the gross receipts tax statements for the past year to make sure they match the income shown on the tax returns. Now is the time to bring in your accountant.

4. Equipment and Inventory. All business sales, especially those involving asset-intensive businesses, warrant an inspection of their hard assets to determine if the inventory is marketable and the equipment is in good repair and adequate for the purposes for which it is intended. Buying any business with obsolete equipment or inventory is like buying a computer without modern software. Beware of sellers insisting that you buy the equipment "as is." This should be considered a *red flag*, and at the very least, require a more extensive inspection of the equipment by a recognized industry expert. Paragraph 5(a) of the Purchase Agreement is designed to protect the buyer from purchasing non-functioning or faulty equipment.

If faced with *leased equipment,* it is important to obtain an assignment of all such leases. This can be a real boon to the buyer if: the equipment lease is nearing the end of its term; it has a cheap buyout provision at the end of the lease period; and the equipment is still viable and productive at that time.

5. Industry Outlook. If you are paying for "goodwill", make sure there is some! Research the industry via the internet to see if it is still a healthy and growing area of commerce. Talk to owners of similar businesses throughout the country to get their feedback. Try to determine where the subject business ranks with respect to its market share and work with the seller to develop a list of the things you can do to improve its position and profitability. If the seller is holding your promissory note, there is strong motivation for the seller to help ensure your future success.

6. Chattel and Tax Lien Search. The closing attorney should order these very important searches to uncover any encumbrances that may exist against the assets of the business which could prevent the closing. Remember, if the seller hasn't been paying the required federal, state and municipal taxes, the reported cash flow is light those respective amounts and the value of the business drops. A smart buyer runs searches on both the business and the owner to make sure all bases are covered.

In some cases these searches will uncover liens that have been paid but have not been released by the creditors. In that event, it will be incumbent upon the seller to notify those creditors and have the liens formally erased in order to provide the buyer some peace of mind. A buyer should require Termination Statements for all such allegedly paid-off liens.

7. Suitable Lease. If you are buying a business with a seven-year promissory note, a three-year lease isn't very protective. The seller's leasehold interests can be transferred to the buyer in one of three ways: (a) a lease assignment, (b) a new lease, or (c) a sublease. If there is plenty of time remaining on the existing lease (renewal options included), it is easier for the seller to simply assign the lease to the buyer, subject to the landlord's approval. If there is only a little time left on the lease, it is often better for the buyer to simply negotiate a new lease with the landlord.

In some instances, the seller may want to sublet the property to the buyer. This only makes sense for a buyer if the buyer can negotiate a lower than current fair market rent, as is the case during recessions and downturns in the commercial real estate market. The following chapter will elaborate further on the art of negotiating a suitable lease.

8. Professional Assistance. A good CPA is necessary to review the financial records, while an experienced business attorney can advise you on legal matters, such as those surrounding important contracts, leases and other agreements. Spending a couple of thousand dollars on professionals, prior to making a major investment, can be a cheap price to pay for peace of mind by eliminating possible negative repercussions.

A couple of year's ago, a distraught gentleman (let's call him Carl), visited my office and related a sad tale. He had recently bought a business directly from an owner and was having serious doubts about its future. When I asked him what due diligence he had performed, he said he had reviewed the profit and loss statements, the lease, the inventory and the equipment. He had also researched the industry to satisfy himself that there was significant growth potential.

Unfortunately, Carl tried to save a buck by using a standard Bill of Sale bought at a stationary store rather than relying on an experienced business broker and attorney to prepare a proper Purchase Agreement, order a chattel and tax lien search and draft the final closing documents. The rest of his story reads like a Steven King novel. Four major pieces of equipment were actually leased and in arrears, the company had not paid any payroll or gross receipts taxes for two years, and there was $20,000 in inventory that was about to be confiscated by the vendor for nonpayment.

Essentially, Carl had purchased a lemon and no amount of post-sale lamenting or posturing was going to turn it into lemonade. Hopefully, Carl's dismal experience will have a positive effect in motivating future buyers to do their pre-sale homework and align themselves with knowledgeable professionals. Due diligence is not just a catchy phrase, it is a requisite for post sale peace of mind.

You only have this one period to review all of the important information you feel is necessary to make the ultimate decision to proceed to a closing. Therefore, use the time wisely by asking your team to help you determine the items you need to review, and above all, to not be afraid to demand the documents they recommend. Following the due diligence period, your earnest money will usually "go hard" (become non-refundable), so spend this time wisely.

CHAPTER THIRTEEN:

THE ALL-IMPORTANT LEASE

At the risk of sounding redundant, I once again address the importance of the Lease. Of course, if you are purchasing the real estate along with the business, this chapter can be skipped.

Location, location, location is an oft-repeated factor that can make or break a small business. In fact, so much attention is paid to getting the right location that once a lease is consummated, it is often filed away like a retired star athlete's jersey. Trouble is, a lease gains in importance with each passing day that brings the tenant closer to its expiration date. That is why its structure is so important to a buyer.

Because one of the primary components of a successful business is a *proven location*, the buyer needs to capitalize on that component by negotiating a suitable lease. The buyer is typically faced with three possibilities in executing a lease: (a) negotiate a new lease with the landlord; (b) obtain a lease assignment from the seller of the business; or (c) sublet the property from the seller. The key consideration in all of these strategies is for the buyer to be able to operate the business, in that proven location, for as many years as the buyer deems necessary and at a fair market rent.

1. Negotiating a new lease. Most sellers prefer that buyers chose this course of action because it enables the seller to eliminate any future responsibilities to the landlord. A new lease is the normal course of action when the current lease (showing the current business owner as tenant) has either expired or has only a small amount of time left before it expires (generally less than two years).

In preparing to negotiate a new lease with the landlord, a buyer should engage the services of a commercial real estate leasing agent to determine the fair market rent for the property and assist in the negotiations. Any commission or fee due the commercial agent is typically paid by the landlord, but if the landlord refuses to compensate the agent, hiring the agent on an hourly fee basis is a whole lot cheaper than signing a bad lease.

Most shopping center leases require the buyer to pay a proportionate share of the center's common area maintenance, property taxes and insurance costs. The percentage is based on the square footage of the business premises as compared to the square footage of the total center. This is called a ***triple-net lease***. Buyers should make sure their real estate agents explain the full impact of all the additional charges and lease obligations.

Rather than sign a long, fixed-term lease, I recommend that a buyer break down the desired length of the lease into segments, such as: one, three-year *fixed term*, followed by two, three-year *renewal options*. This provides the buyer with a guaranteed nine years in the proven location, but with the right to terminate the lease at the end of each three-year segment if the existing location proves undesirable, another location becomes more desirable or the buyer decides to become a seller.

Several years ago (yep, another anecdote), I was asked to sell a franchised flower shop. In order to guarantee a long-term presence at the chosen location, the *franchisor*, not the franchisee, signed a thirty-year, fixed-term lease with onerous rent escalators. The franchisee was required to assume the lease, along with its long-term responsibilities, via a lease assignment. After four years, the franchisee decided to sell the business because it wasn't providing the return she had anticipated. Unfortunately, no buyer wanted to assume a fixed-term lease with twenty-six years remaining. The business eventually sold for only $8,000.00 (the inventory value) despite being valued at more than $175,000.00. The buyer felt the *fire-sale* price justified the long-term risk…while the seller was just grateful to get out from under a lease obligation that could have cost her nearly one million dollars before it expired.

When negotiations begin on a *new* lease, the landlord will often ask for a large increase in rent to bring the property up to current market rent. Such a major increase in rent will obviously distort the cash flow that the buyer is relying upon in purchasing the business. If a rent increase is appropriate, in order to keep the deal on track the buyer can ask for a "stair-step" increase, whereby a targeted overall increase is achieved in stages, with the rent at the tail-end of the lease increased to offset the lower than market rent at the onset of the new lease.

Leases will often contain automatic rent escalators to enable the rent to keep pace with inflation. Some of these escalators are in the form of the Consumer Price Index (CPI) which is a national standard used by many banks in determining the rate of inflation. To protect both landlord and tenant, the CPI can be bracketed, e.g., CPI increases of no less than two percent and no more than five percent per year. An optional method is to set a fixed increase expressed in dollars per square foot, e.g., an increase of $1.00 per square foot per year, or as a fixed percentage, e.g., three percent per year. Most leases today are *triple-net leases* that guarantee landlords a fixed base rent while charging the tenant for its proportionate share of the property taxes, maintenance and insurance. [See the sample Commercial Lease Agreement on page 58].

2. The lease assignment. When more than one or two years remain on the current lease, the landlord may not be interested in executing a new lease with the buyer, choosing instead to add the buyer to the current lease alongside the seller. In a lease assignment, the buyer agrees to assume all the duties and responsibilities called for in the lease through its current term. This includes the existing rent schedule and triple-net charges. Under this scenario, the seller remains on the lease through its original term, and in the event the buyer defaults on the lease, the seller is still the responsible party. This gives the landlord an increased measure of security because there are two tenants on the lease instead of only one. However, under this scenario, the seller is justifiably concerned over the lingering obligation to the landlord. [See the sample Lease Assignment on page 63].

3. Subleasing. A sublease occurs when the original tenant (the business owner/seller), becomes the *landlord* by leasing the premises to a third party (the buyer). Under this scenario, the seller remains solely responsible for all the terms and conditions of the lease while the buyer becomes responsible for only those terms and conditions that the seller imposes in the sublease. Often these terms and conditions are similar to those in the original lease.

A sublease is most often used when a tenant decides to vacate a space prior to the expiration of the lease. In some cases, in order for the current tenant (the seller) to be able to rent the property, the sublease may be at a lower rent than the original lease...which is obviously in the best interest of the new tenant (the buyer). A sublease is the least common method of taking over a business premises because it generally requires the landlord's approval and most landlords don't relish the thought of losing control over the premises.

4. Month-to-month leases. If a business owner's lease is getting close to expiration and a decision has been made to sell the business, I often advise the would-be seller to ask the landlord for a month-to-month lease until a buyer is found. This allows the seller to be free of any post-sale lease responsibilities because it will require a new lease to be signed by the buyer of the business. In most cases landlords will grant this relief to the seller especially if the seller has been a good tenant; and sometimes a landlord will allow month-to-month status only if the seller will guarantee the new lease for a short period of time. Either option is preferable to the seller having to sign a new long-term lease and accept a lease assignment.

CHAPTER FOURTEEN:

COMMERCIAL LEASE AGREEMENT

[Here's a sample triple net lease for your review. Please note that any/all segments of the sample lease are negotiable and should be discussed with a commercial real estate attorney]

This lease is made between _____(legal entity)_____ of _____(address)_____, herein called Lessor and _____(legal entity)_____, herein called Lessee. Lessee hereby offers to lease from Lessor the premises situated in the City of _____, County of _____, State of _____, described as ____(business name)____, containing approximately _____ square feet, and hereinafter referred to as the "demised premises," upon the following TERMS and CONDITIONS:

1. Term of Lease and Renewal Options.
This Lease is for _____ (__) months beginning _____ and ending _____. The term of the Lease, if then in full force and effect and if Lessee shall have performed all the terms, conditions and covenants thereof, may be extended, at the option of Lessee, for _____ (__) additional months, beginning _____ and terminating on _____. Lessee shall give written notice to Lessor of its intent to exercise such option to extend no later than _____ (__) days prior to the expiration of the initial term of the Lease.

2. Rent.
Lessee does hereby covenant and agree to pay, as rent in advance on the first day of each rental month, without notice and demand, the sum of _____ and No/100 dollars ($_____.00) for the period from _____ to _____. The Lease rate for options will be the prevailing market rate for similar type buildings as negotiated by both parties in good faith. At no time will the rate increase be less than

__% nor more than __% per renewal option. Rents received after the fifth (5th) day of each month will be considered late. Lessee agrees to pay Lessor a $_____.00 late fee for each late rent payment.

3. Use.
Lessee shall use and occupy the demised premises for the purpose of _____ _____ and related activities. The demised premises shall be used for no other purpose without the prior written consent of Lessor. Lessee shall not use the demised premises for storing, manufacturing or selling any explosives, flammables, or other inherently dangerous or toxic substances, materials, chemicals, things or devices.

4. Care and Maintenance of Premises.
Lessee acknowledges that the demised premises are in good order and repair, unless other-wise indicated herein. Lessee will, at its own expense and at all times, maintain the demised premises in good and safe condition, including all plate glass, electrical wiring, plumbing and heating installations and any other system or equipment in or upon the demised premises, and shall surrender the same, at termination hereof, in as good condition as received, normal wear and tear excepted. In the event removal of equipment attached to the building is necessary for any reason, lessee agrees to restore building to as close to its original condition as possible. Lessee will be responsible for all repairs and maintenance required, including but not limited to fixtures and heating and cooling units, misuse, waste or neglect of that of its employees or visitors. Lessor will be responsible for all structural maintenance to include the roof, exterior walls and structural foundations. Lessee shall be responsible for any damage caused to the demised premises by Lessee's negligence and that of Lessee's employees and visitors.

5. Alterations.
Lessee shall not, without first obtaining the written consent of Lessor, make any alterations, additions, or improvements in, to, or about the demised premises.

6. Ordinances and Statutes.
Lessee shall comply with all statutes, ordinances and requirements of

all municipal, state and federal authorities now in force and which may hereafter be in force, pertaining to the demised premises, occasioned by or affecting the use thereof by Lessee.

7. Assignment and Subletting.
Lessee shall not assign this Lease or sublet any portion of the demised premises without the prior written consent of Lessor, which shall not be unreasonably withheld. Any such assignment or subletting without the prior written consent shall be void and, at the sole option of Lessor, may terminate this lease.

8. Utilities.
All applications and connections for necessary utility services on the demised premises shall be made in the name of Lessee only, and Lessee shall be liable for utility charges as they become due, including sewer, water, gas, electricity, internet access and telephone services. Lessee further acknowledges that the demised premises are designed to provide standard electrical service and standard lighting for normal usage and currently installed equipment. Lessee shall not use any equipment or devices that utilize excessive electrical energy, or that may, in Lessor's reasonable opinion, overload the wiring or interfere with electrical services.

9. Entry and Inspection.
Lessee shall permit Lessor or Lessor's agent(s) to enter the demised premises at reasonable times and upon reasonable notice, for the purpose of inspecting the same, and shall permit Lessor at any time within sixty (60) days prior to the expiration of this Lease, to place upon the demised premises any usual "To Let", "For Lease" or "For Sale" signs, and permit prospective lessees or purchasers desiring to lease the same to inspect the demised premises thereafter.

10. Parking.
During the term of this Lease, Lessee shall have the exclusive use of automobile parking areas, driveways, and footways, subject to rules and regulations for the use thereof as prescribed from time to time by Lessor.

11. Indemnification of Lessor.
To the extent permitted by law, Lessor shall not be liable for any

damage or injury to Lessee, or any other person, or to any property, occurring on the demised premises or any
part thereof. Lessee agrees to indemnify and hold Lessor harmless from any claims for damages which arise in connection with any such occurrence. Said indemnification shall include indemnity from all costs or fees which Lessor may incur in defending said claim.

12. Insurance.
Lessee, at its expense, shall maintain plate glass and public liability insurance, including bodily injury and property damage, insuring Lessee and Lessor with minimum coverage as follows: coverage limits of not less than $_____.00 for each person and $_____.00 in the aggregate for bodily injury or death liability for each accident, and $_____.00 for property damage liability for each accident, for the benefit of both Lessor and Lessee as protection against all liability claims arising from the premises. Lessee shall provide Lessor with a Certificate of Insurance showing Lessor as additional insured. The Certificate shall provide for a ten-day written notice to Lessor in the event of a cancellation or material change of coverage. To the maximum extent permitted by insurance policies which may be owned by Lessor or Lessee, Lessee and Lessor, for the benefit of each other, waive any and all rights of subrogation which may otherwise exist. If the demised premises or any other part of the building is damaged by fire or other casualty resulting from any act of negligence of Lessee or any of Lessee's agents, employees or invitees, rent shall not be diminished or abated while such damages are under repair, and Lessee shall be responsible for costs of repair not covered by insurance.

13. Eminent Domain.
If the demised premises, or any part thereof or any estate therein, or any other part of the building materially affecting Lessee's use of the demised premises, shall be taken by eminent domain, this lease shall terminate on the date when title vests pursuant to such taking. The rent, and any additional rent, shall be apportioned as of the termination date, and any rent paid for any period beyond that date shall be repaid to Lessee. Lessee shall not be entitled to any part of the award for such taking or any payment in lieu thereof, but Lessee may file a claim for any taking of fixtures and improvements owned

by Lessee, and for moving expenses and will negotiate in good faith payment for any other expense.

14. Destruction of Premises. Lessee shall give Lessor immediate notice in case of fire or other damage or casualty to the demised premises, or any part thereof. In the event of partial destruction of the demised premises during the term hereof, from any cause, Lessee shall forthwith repair the same. Lessee shall maintain, at its own expense, an insurance policy in force for the premises in the amount of no less than $_____.00. Lessee shall provide Lessor with a Certificate of Insurance showing Lessor as additional insured and beneficiary.

15. Lessor's Remedies on Default.
If any default is made in the payment of rent, or any part thereof, at the times hereinbefore specified, or if any default is made in the performance of or compliance with any of the other terms or conditions hereof, this Lease, at the option of Lessor and to the extent permitted by law, shall terminate and be forfeited, and Lessor may re-enter the demised premises and remove all persons there to the extent permitted by law.

16. Common Area Expenses, Property Taxes and Insurance costs.
Lessee agrees to pay $_____.00 per month for maintenance of the grounds and cleaning of property. Parking lot resealing and marking will be the responsibility of the Lessor. Common area maintenance will include: clean up of exterior, maintenance of parking lot, snow removal, landscape maintenance and weed control.

17. Property Taxes.
Property Taxes are the responsibility of the Lessee and will be paid in full within 15 days of presenting of bill by Lessor. Payment terms extended by _____ County will be automatically extended to Lessee and Lessee, at its own discretion, may elect to pay such taxes in full as cash flow permits.

18. Attorney's Fees.
In case suit should be brought for recovery of the demised premises or

for any sum due hereunder, or because of any act which may arise out of the possession of the demised premises, by either party, the prevailing party shall be entitled to all costs incurred in connection with such action, including reasonable attorney's fees and court costs.

19. Waiver.
No failure of Lessor to enforce any term hereof shall be deemed to be a waiver.

20. Notices.
All notices pursuant to this agreement shall be in writing and addressed as follows.

To "Landlord":   To "Tenant":

_____   _____

_____   _____

21. Heirs, Assigns, Successors.
This Lease is binding upon and inures to the benefit of the heirs, assigns and successors in interest to the parties.

22. Subordination.
This Lease is and shall be subordinated to all existing and future liens and encumbrances against the property.

23. Right of First Refusal.
In the event Lessor receives a bona fide and acceptable offer to purchase the demised premises from a third party, Lessor shall immediate notify the Lessee of the terms of said offer and Lessee shall have Thirty (30) days in which to agree to match the third party offer and notify Seller of such intent with a signed purchase agreement. If Lessee fails to notify Lessor of such intent within the stated period, Lessor will be free to accept the third party offer and consummate the sale of the property.

24. Entire Agreement.
The foregoing constitutes the entire agreement between the parties

and may be modified only in a written amendment signed by both parties.

25. Liability.
Lessor shall not be liable for any loss, expense or damage to any person or property. Lessee is responsible for all acts or negligence of Lessee's employees, visitors or invitees.

26. Choice of Law.
This lease shall be governed by the laws of the State of _____, and all disputes shall be subject to the jurisdiction of the Courts of the State of _____.

IN WITNESS WHEREOF, the parties have executed this lease on _____, 20__ and have each received a copy of the executed Lease.

_____
Lessor

_____
Lessee

Signed in the presence of:

_____

NOTICE: State law establishes rights and obligations for parties to rental agreements. If you have a question about the interpretation or legality of a provision of this agreement, you should seek assistance from a lawyer or other qualified person in your state. Contact your local county real estate board for additional forms that may be required to meet your specific needs.

CHAPTER FIFTEEN:

THE LEASE ASSIGNMENT

[Some Lease Assignments require a notary public to witness the signatures of both the buyer and seller - the landlord's signature does not generally have to be notarized]

For valuable consideration, we do hereby assign, set over and transfer unto _____(Buyer)_____ (herein, the "Assignee"), all of our rights, title and interest in and to that certain Lease dated _____, 20____, between _____ (herein, the "Landlord"), and _____ (herein, the "Tenant"), covering the premises located at _____ (Address) _____(City, State, Zip)_____, known as _____(Business Name)_____, and subject to the same terms and conditions of the Lease therein set out, which the Assignee hereby assumes and agrees to perform all the covenants, terms, and conditions of said Lease on the part of the Tenant therein named to be performed.

Dated this ___th day of _____, 20___.

STATE OF _____) Tenant
) ss.   _____
COUNTY OF _____) Tenant

The foregoing instrument was acknowledged before me this ___th day of _____, 20__, by_____.

My Commission Expires: _____._____
                                                             Notary Public

CONSENT OF ASSIGNEE

I/We, _____(Buyer)_____ do hereby accept the foregoing Assignment and hereby assume and agree to perform all of the terms, covenants and conditions of the Lease therein described on the part of the Tenant therein named to be performed. It is understood and agreed, that in the event the purchase of the business known as _____ is not consummated, this acceptance of the foregoing Assignment is null and void.

Dated this ____th day of _____, 20__.

STATE OF _____)
) ss.
COUNTY OF _____)

_____
Buyer/Assignee

_____
Buyer/Assignee Tenant

The foregoing instrument was acknowledged before me this ___the day of _____, 20__, by _____.

My Commission Expires: _____._____
                                                                            Notary Public

CONSENT OF LANDLORD

The above Assignment is consented to by the undersigned Landlord, upon the condition, however, that the said Assignment shall not release, relieve, or in any manner modify the obligations of _____(Seller)_____, Tenant, under the terms and conditions of said Lease.

Dated this ___th day of _____, 20__.

By:_____   _____
      Landlord   Attest

CHAPTER SIXTEEN:

CLOSING THE SALE

Once due diligence has been completed and all contingencies satisfied, the sale can move forward to a closing. This generally requires the services of an escrow attorney who takes the compact Purchase Agreement and creates a multi-page set of closing documents that contain all of the legal verbiage required by our litigious society.

I suggest the use of a *neutral* escrow attorney who is willing to prepare reasonable and fair closing documents with no bias towards either party. To maintain that neutrality, the attorney's fee should be split equally between buyer and seller. Currently (circa 2014), the total fee typically runs about $1,500 to $2,000 depending upon the size of the transaction.

Prior to closing, here is a list of activities that must be addressed:

a) The buyer must make sure there is a lease prepared, on terms and conditions specified in the Purchase Agreement, and set to commence immediately upon closing.

b) The buyer and seller should inspect and count the inventory (if applicable) to ensure that it is equal to the amount called for in the Purchase Agreement. In the event the inventory is either more or less than stated in the Purchase Agreement, the purchase price and down payment (or promissory note) should be adjusted accordingly.

c) The buyer must make arrangements for the necessary funds to be on hand, which can take days if the money is in investments that must be liquidated. A cashier's check or money order, made out to the escrow attorney's trust fund, will likely be required.

d) The buyer must obtain a business license from the local governing body. If the business entity is a restaurant or bar, other licenses may be required which may take several weeks to acquire.

e) The buyer must also obtain the necessary state and federal tax identification numbers.

f) The buyer needs to make sure that there is a general liability insurance policy in effect at time of closing. In most cases, the buyer and seller will contact the seller's insurance company and ask that the buyer be added to the policy that is already in existence through its current term. This procedure saves precious time as the closing date approaches.

g) As part of his closing responsibilities, the escrow attorney should order chattel and tax lien searches to determine if there are any liens, judgments or other encumbrances that might prevent the transfer of "free and clear" assets to the buyer. If the buyer and seller and their respective attorneys approve the final closing documents, and the searches reveal no encumbrances, the deal can close.

h) If the business is located in a state that has a gross receipts tax or some other general sales tax, the escrow attorney should prepare a *tax clearance* request that transfers the responsibility of collecting and paying that tax from the seller to the buyer.

Immediately after closing:

a) The buyer needs to contact the various utilities to transfer service.

b) The buyer should reimburse the seller for any prepaid business expenses such as rent, utilities and insurance.

c) The purchase of a manufacturing business may require

negotiating the work-in-progress. In most of these situations, the buyer reimburses the seller for any expenses the seller has incurred for the work-in-progress that exists at time of closing. The buyer and seller typically agree to divide the profits from the work in progress, with the buyer receiving the larger percentage.

d) If vehicles are involved in the sale of the business, the buyer and seller should get the titles to the vehicles changed over to the buyer as soon as possible after the closing.

A well-executed transaction will preclude the business's employees knowing about the takeover until after the closing. This is important in order to prevent the likelihood of employees "jumping ship" in the belief that the new owner will likely be impossible to work for or will replace them all with friends and relatives. When the buyer and seller address the employees after the closing, the buyer has the advantage of being able to present himself or herself in the most favorable light, letting the employees know that their continued support will be greatly appreciated and rewarded with long-term employment opportunities. It doesn't hurt for the buyer to bring donuts or other treats to the meeting or for the seller to take everyone to lunch after the introduction in order to celebrate the sale.

CHAPTER SEVENTEEN:

AVOIDING THE POST-PURCHASE BLUES

Buying a business can be stressful, especially when you are entering an industry or profession in which you possess limited knowledge or experience. Initially, your time is consumed by the rigors of training and little thought is given to the pitfalls new business owners may encounter if they don't plan ahead. Here are some steps that can be taken to reduce post-sale stress. The names are fictitious but the events actually took place as described.

1. **Know your key customers and vendors**. Following the closing, ask the seller to immediately arrange face-to-face meetings with these key people, especially if you have exclusive or semi-exclusive agreements in place.

    In a past sale of a supply business, the purchaser acquired three exclusive product lines that were all integral to the company's continued success. Each product line had a long and successful history with the company and was represented by trained sales people. Following some earnest lobbying by the seller, the three suppliers agreed to maintain their exclusive status with the buyer on a probationary basis. Unfortunately, seven months later, the new owner discovered that one of her sales people was cutting his bid margins so thin that the company was actually losing money on some of his jobs. When confronted with the problem, the salesman got mad and quit, threatening to take his product line with him. Fortunately, through personal contacts, phone calls and emails, the new owner developed a personal relationship with the key supplier in the months following the sale and was able to retain the product line despite this serious threat.

2. **Create a budget and a comprehensive accounting system**. Running a small business without an understandable plan and accounting system is like trying to sail a ship without a rudder.

Too many business owners receive their monthly income statements, check out only the "bottom line" to see if they made any money, and toss them into a file. It's important to pay close attention to every major budget deviation, especially as they pertain to the cost of materials and payroll.

Randy bought a cabinet shop and within the first six months his payroll costs were soaring in comparison to sales. Upon further inspection, Randy discovered that in his haste to get product out the door, he was incurring huge overtime charges that severely impacted his profit margin. A frank meeting with his shop foreman quickly corrected the situation. Randy was simply being tested by his employees.

You will also want to keep a wary eye on both the age and amount of your accounts receivable and accounts payable. Accounts receivable that are more than forty-five days old spell trouble. On the other hand, early payment of your accounts receivable may result in some attractive discounts…often as much as five percent. Also, be sure to ask your CPA to highlight any aberrations on your monthly financial statement that he or she feels should come to your attention. The best CPA is one who can spot problems in your business before they become destructive.

3. **Make changes slowly**. I typically advise new owners to spend at least six to eight months learning their new business before making any sweeping changes. There is a tendency for new owners to want to make major changes in order to release the "vast potential" that so enticingly looms on the horizon. Resist that initial urge or the unrealized "potential" may become nothing more than a mirage.

Bill was just such an owner. Following a month of training from the seller, Bill decided to flex his own entrepreneurial muscles by "simplifying" his company's price list. However, Bill was an ex-government employee who simplified his price list the way the IRS periodically simplifies the tax code. Bill's customers were not amused, and although many would have profited from new volume discounts, his changes were more irritating than stimulating. Bill should have consulted with the seller before making such a major strategic change. That's why there is a consulting provision in the purchase agreement.

The Romans espoused the philosophy, *festina lente* (make haste slowly) and they conquered the known world. By exercising a bit of caution and planning, you should be able to conquer your new entrepreneurial world.

4. **Assess your own capabilities**. Some of us see ourselves as gregarious and friendly, when in reality we should be down in the lube pit and let a more affable employee greet customers and write invoices.

   Jeff and Tina bought a service business through me that required extensive customer contact. Jeff decided to work the production side of the business while Tina covered the front counter. After their second week in business, the seller (who was training the couple) alerted me to the fact that Tina was driving customers away with her surly attitude. When I tactfully broached the subject with Jeff, he replied, "I know, but what can I do? She's my wife so I can't just fire her." But after three more weeks, in the wake of increasing customer complaints and declining sales, Tina was in the back office doing the bookkeeping while Jeff was at the front counter greeting customers.

5. **Nurture key employees**. If the business is sailing smoothly, don't replace the people at the helm or in the rigging, i.e. *if it isn't broke, don't break it!*

   Marilyn, the owner of a small manufacturing business, discovered that lesson the hard way when she decided to personally replace her experienced production manager. Within days the plant was running behind schedule and the money Marilyn was saving in payroll was more than offset by plummeting sales. Good employees, like derby winners, are extremely hard to find and expensive to train, so treat them like a precious resource and try to overlook their idiosyncrasies.

CHAPTER EIGHTEEN:

GUERILLA CASH FLOW MANAGEMENT

Regardless of how well you run your business, there are times, e.g., recessions, when cash *flow* becomes a *trickle* and you have to scramble to survive. After interviewing scores of New Mexico business owners on the subject, here is a compilation of their survival tactics:

1. Create a reserve. During good times, at least *consider* the possibility of a downturn in the economy and stash some cash. Many business consultants suggest a six-month reserve, but at least try to have three months of operating capital stowed away in the event a rainy day turns into a deluge. Some of the most successful entrepreneurs have proffered the advice that the real fortunes are made during recessions. But you need a decent cash reserve to take advantage of those opportunities.

2. Aggressively trim expenses. Take out your annual budget and monthly profit and loss statements and examine every expense category for possible savings. No business owner enjoys paring payroll, but it is sometimes necessary to save the company. Some expenses, such as rent, utilities, insurance and taxes cannot be eliminated without potentially dire consequences. However, be very wary of cutting too much out of your advertising budget (often a favorite target) because you need sales to survive. A desperate entrepreneur should be able to trim at lease some fat from auto expenses, supplies, travel and entertainment. **Never** stop paying your payroll and gross receipts taxes. In the tragic event you must file for bankruptcy, these important tax obligations <u>are not</u> discharged…so they follow you like a barnacle on a boat.

3. Offer early payment discounts. If your business carries accounts receivable, contact your customers and offer them discounts if they pay in ten days or less. A two percent to five percent discount off a $5,000 invoice may create an "urgency" on the part of your customers while helping you out of a cash bind.

4. Talk to your vendors. If your vendors have been in business for more than a few years, they have likely experienced their own cash flow difficulties, and as a result, have amassed comfortable cash reserves. Sometimes, a simple telephone call explaining your situation and requesting a little more time to pay can result in a sympathetic moratorium on an overdue bill, especially if you offer to pay some interest on the outstanding debt. Remember, your personal contact means a great deal to a vendor. It means you are taking a pro-active role in solving your cash flow problems rather than waiting for the vendor to send you repetitive invoices without a response. If you're in business for the long haul, maintaining a friendly and respectful relationship with your vendors is imperative.

5. Consider leasing. If you need a new piece of equipment to get you out of your cash flow jam (e.g., to reduce labor costs and/or increase productivity), try leasing rather than buying. Many leasing companies offer rent-to-own programs that allow you to purchase a piece of equipment at the end of the lease period. The cost of leasing a piece of new equipment must always be compared to purchasing that same piece, over time, through bank asset-lending programs.

6. **Talk to your creditors.** If you have a seller-held note, a bank loan or line of credit, discuss your situation with your creditors. No seller or banker wants to write-off a loan, so most will work with you to help find a satisfactory solution to your problem. Request an interest-only moratorium until you can get the business back on track. Remember, the *golden rule* in dealing with your creditors in crisis situations is **communicate**! Like most key people in your business life, creditors don't want to be ignored. Treat them with respect and they will have reason to respect both you and your requests…they simply want to know that they will eventually be paid.

7. Hold an inventory *fire sale*. Recently, a friend of mine with a "financially-troubled" manufacturing business asked me to sell it because he thought that was his only option. Instead of holding a *fire sale* for his **business**, I convinced him to fire-sale his old and obsolete **inventory**. Amazingly, he was able to sell off more than $50,000.00 worth of unimportant inventory he thought was unmarketable. EBay offers yet another venue for manufacturers, wholesalers and retailers to "dump" unwanted inventories and free-up valuable cash. This same strategy applies to old furniture, fixtures and equipment that have outlived their usefulness but may still be a low-cost salvation to fellow entrepreneurs.

8. Empower your employees, friends and family. Before you throw in the towel, have a frank discussion with your employees. Ask them for their ideas on how to cut costs and possibly offer ownership interests to those who are willing to contribute their personal funds to keep the company afloat during the tough times. Employees who invest in their company generally maintain a strong emotional and financial attachment. Employee contributions can come in the form of either cash investments or reduced wages. Friends and family should also be surveyed to see if any "arm-chair" entrepreneurs are willing to invest.

9. Talk to your landlord. During economic downturns, prudent landlords are often willing to adjust the rent in order to preserve a tenant because tenants paying some rent are far better than having to lease an empty office, storefront or factory during an economic downturn. During the most recent recession, tenants were able to obtain significant rent reductions in return for extending their leases and agreeing to pay a higher rent once the economic tide turned.

10. Revisit past customers. Offer past customers discounts for new purchases along with incentives to refer you to their relatives, friends and associates. And most importantly, nurture your existing customer base by visiting them (when possible) and expressing your appreciation for their business.

11. As a last resort...Factoring. Several Albuquerque finance companies will factor accounts receivable, i.e., lend money in exchange for a secured interest in a company's accounts receivable. I consider factoring a last resort measure due to the high interest rates that generally apply. If factoring becomes a company's modus operandi rather than a last gasp measure, it can contribute to the eventual demise of the business. However, when your ship is sinking, you reach out for anything that floats.

Essential to any course of action is to have a realistic plan in place for the usage of any funds (or concessions) you receive. Few vendors, bankers, employees, friends or even family members will assist you without a reasonable expectation that your business will survive the current crisis and eventually prosper enough to repay them.

Wayne J. Unze
BUSINESS CONSULTANT & APPRAISER

PART TWO:
HOW TO RETIRE IN STYLE

INTRODUCTION

One of the hardest things an entrepreneur eventually faces is the eventual sale or liquidation of the business's assets. A business, unlike a home or investment property, generally holds a stronger emotional attachment because it requires the owner's blood, sweat and tears to grow and prosper. Getting through this emotional rollercoaster ride is extremely difficult for many sellers because it compares with putting one's baby up for adoption. That is why proper planning and execution are so important.

The grand myth is that businesses are only offered for sale when they are in dire financial straits. However, unless there's a recession, that is the least cited reason for a sale. Most sellers decide on divestiture as a logical course of action when faced with one of the following:

> 1. **The "Dismal D's"** (disability, divorce, death, dissention or declining market). Disability and death are obvious reasons for a sale. A divorce may result in a court-ordered forced sale of the business to satisfy the division of the couple's assets. Employee dissention can create such stress that the business becomes unmanageable and a strategic divestitures may be the only way to maintain the owner's sanity. In a declining market, as a result of limited product acceptance or a diminishing customer base, owners may also be faced with the stark reality of divestiture.
>
> 2. **Health.** Lingering ill health is one of the most often cited reasons for an owner wishing to sell as well as being a strong motivational factor for a quick transaction. The key is not to wait until the illness makes working impossible. A successful divestiture takes stamina, both physical and psychological.
>
> 3. **Retirement**. Reaching the "golden years" is a strong reason for a planned divestiture, especially if the business has been a financial success and will afford the owner a desirable

retirement life-style.

4. **Burnout and stress**. These can be killers, both from a physical as well as a business perspective. Business owners who can't stand the heat should get out of the kitchen as soon as possible. They certainly shouldn't wait until stress has created more serious health problems.

5. **Trading up**. One way for an entrepreneur to improve his or her lot is to sell a small business in order to acquire a larger enterprise.

6. **Relocation.** When a spouse receives a job transfer, it can trigger a cause for a quick sale...or possibly result in a divorce. Choosing to divest of the business, and not the spouse, is cheaper and far less stressful!

Fortunately, there is a proven pathway to a successful divestiture if you choose to take it. Information is the key to accomplishing a successful divestiture and you can garner a great deal of the necessary information in the "How to Become an Entrepreneur" section of this book. Before attempting to negotiate the sale or purchase of any business, it is imperative that both buyers and sellers understand each others' desires, fears and motivations – which is why I included both sides of the entrepreneurial coin in this book. I strongly advise you to read both parts of this book for the best possible outcome in your quest to sell. You will notice that some chapters are duplicated in both sections. This is due to the fact that those chapters have <u>special</u> significance for both the buyer and seller.

My motivation for writing this book stems from the thousands of buyers and sellers I interviewed over my thirty-year career and the costly mistakes so many made in the pursuit of their financial and social goals. It is my deepest desire that this book be used as a road map to prevent would-be buyers and sellers from repeating those financially destructive mistakes.

The Chapters dealing with Valuing a Business, the Nondisclosure Agreement and the Asset Purchase Agreement have been duplicated in both sections of this book because they are chapters that are vitally important to both the buying and selling process.

CHAPTER ONE:

PREPARING A BUSINESS FOR SALE

Like most complex transactions, the devil is in the details. Overlook one and your sale can become a disaster, both financially and mentally. To avoid the pitfalls of an errant business sale, the first step is to hire an experienced team of advisors:

1. A business broker to appraise the business, develop a defensible sale price and reasonable terms, and discreetly market the business to qualified prospects.

2. An accountant to suggest ways to minimize taxes, analyze the buyer's financial statement and provide any other financial advice needed by the team.

3. A business-oriented attorney to provide the necessary legal assistance by reviewing both the purchase agreement and final closing documents.

It will be the business broker's responsibility to qualify each potential buyer and assure a high level of confidentiality throughout the selling process. It is vital that the business's customers, vendors, employees and competitors are not made aware that the business is for sale. If word leaks out, customers tend to believe they will not receive any post-sale support; vendors have a tendency to put the seller on a COD basis; employees get nervous and may start looking for new employment; and competitors will tell the world that the seller is "going out of business." All four of these situations can harm the businesses by making it less attractive to potential buyers.

The business broker will also be the person to help the team develop a marketing and pricing strategy, assist in negotiating a win-win transaction and create the purchase agreement that will cement the deal. Using an experienced business broker to negotiate on your behalf keeps personalities and emotions out of the mix, which makes for better objectivity. Sellers who try to negotiate their own deals will often feel insulted if a buyer makes a disparaging remark about the business. An experienced business broker, on the other hand, will unemotionally counter the remark with concise, factual information and keep the deal on track.

The accountant's job is to assist the team in updating the business's books and records and resolving any tax, contractual or other financial problems. The buyer's accountant will want to see tax records along with current income statements and balance sheets and it will fall upon the seller's accountant to have these documents available. It will also be the responsibility of the seller's accountant to review the buyer's financial statement and credit report and advise the seller as to the credit-worthiness of the buyer, especially if the seller is asked to carry back a promissory note from the buyer.

The attorney's role is to settle any pending litigation in order to free the business's assets from any encumbrances that might hinder the consummation of a sale. The attorney is also responsible for reviewing and advising the seller regarding any and all contracts that need to be signed. The attorney may also want to order a tax lien search and chattel search, prior to putting the business on the market, to make sure there are no outstanding liens that would prevent the seller from conveying clear title to all of the assets. It should be noted that many promissory notes, equipment leases and other pledges of collateral are seldom removed from the public records after they have been paid. These outstanding liens will usually show up in the Chattel Search and can delay a sale until they are removed with a Termination Statement.

Prior to marketing the business, the seller should remove all nonessential or personal effects from the premises so there are no misconceptions as to what assets actually go with the business. For example, I once witnessed a buyer and seller arguing at length over a sailfish that was mounted above the seller's desk and spotted by the buyer during the due diligence process, but removed by the seller immediately prior to the closing. The buyer was willing to take such drastic steps as to rescind the sale if the sailfish wasn't returned. Fortunately, the seller was seeing things more clearly and acquiesced even though the mounting wasn't part of the assets conveyed in the Purchase Agreement.

The seller is further charged with the task of training the buyer after the sale, so the development of a Training Manual can be a giant step in that direction and make the ownership transition much easier. It is also a good idea for the seller to assemble a list of customers and vendors which the buyer will expect to receive at closing.

If the business has broken-down or obsolete equipment, it should be repaired or replaced prior to the business being placed on the market. Buyers want to believe that they have purchased an ongoing and viable business with all its components intact. Inoperable equipment sends a red flag that will create immediate concern for the buyer and a loss of credibility for the seller. The same is true of the phrase, "as is." An equipment list, with estimated current market values (in the current used condition) should also be developed so it can be included in the marketing package. If there is leased equipment, the leases should be assembled for the buyer's review during the due diligence process.

The leasehold interest is one of the most important non-tangible assets to be transferred at closing, so now is a good time to review it so you will know what to expect from both the buyer and your landlord. If you have a year or less left on your lease, you have a couple of choices: ask your landlord for one or more renewal options that will benefit the buyer but not bind you after your original term is over; or tell the landlord you intend to provide an introduction to the buyer so the landlord can strike a deal on a long-term lease that will go into effect at closing and remove all of the seller's future lease obligations. For more leasehold interest information, please see Chapter 16 (page 55).

This is also a good time to look at the physical attractiveness of the business and make any cosmetic improvements you feel will make the business more attractive and welcoming. The final major step in preparing a business for sale is to determine both a defensible and realistic selling price and terms.

CHAPTER TWO:

VALUING A BUSINESS

Over the years I have encountered scores of would-be business buyers and sellers who had one critical shortcoming: they didn't know how to calculate a realistic value for the business they were determined to buy or sell. Unfortunately, in many of these cases they went ahead with the purchase or sale and suffered some tragic consequences. Essentially, their emotions won out over sound logic. A defensible evaluation is the foundation for all the other components of the buying and selling process. It is also the most subjective part of the buying and selling process, requiring both investigative and cognitive skills.

The primary requisite in valuing a business is discovering its true *cash flow*. **I define *cash flow* as: the money that remains unspent after all the <u>necessary</u> expenses of the businesses have been satisfied but before the owner has been compensated and before any debt has been serviced.** As a means of discovery, I question sellers about <u>every</u> expense category to determine if an expense is a true business expense or a *personal* expense, e.g., the owner's auto expenses, personal travel, or health insurance premiums. I caution sellers that anything deemed "personal" in nature, must be provable. For example, a personal health insurance expense should be backed up with cancelled checks or credit card receipts. I also look specifically for any expenses considered to be non-recurring, such as one-time moving expenses or paid-off equipment leases - all these expenses can be considered part of (added to) the *cash flow*.

As part of my *discovery process*, I also compare every expense category on the seller's tax return to the same expense categories in the previous three years and I require explanations about any major aberrations I find (these same questions will likely be asked by either the buyer or the buyer's accountant during due diligence).

Here's a typical case study from a buyer's perspective. A few years ago I was contacted by a lady who wanted me to "coach" her regarding the acquisition of a retail business in a popular Texas tourist area. The seller was asking $1.2 million for both his business and its real estate. Rachael (not her real name) had already *emotionally* purchased the long-established boutique, but to her credit, she wanted some price verification before making an offer.

In order to evaluate the business, I asked Rachael to get me the following information (the same data I require in most of the evaluations I develop):

1. The last three years of the business's year-end profit and loss statements (P&L's), balance sheets, and tax returns, as well as its most recent P&L and balance sheet;

2. Existing real estate and equipment leases;

3. Existing mortgages on real estate or promissory notes encumbering the *chattel* (an old English term for *tangible assets*);

5 Franchise Disclosure Document (if the business is a franchise);

14. Furniture, fixtures and equipment list (with the seller's best estimate of the current fair market value of the major items);

15. Best estimate of the business's normal inventory level, i.e. the amount of inventory necessary to sustain the operation on a daily basis (at seller's cost);

16. History of the business showing its chain of ownership, any past or pending litigation and the owner's future growth strategies;

17. The business's legal structure: sole proprietor, Sub-chapter S or C corporation, Limited Liability Company (LLC), or

partnership;

18. Employee information (years with the company, duties, wages and benefits);

19. Description of the business facility: location, zoning, size of the building and lot, and any special features (docks, overhead doors, ceiling height, shelving, cranes, paving, fencing, power sources, heating and cooling systems, etc.);

20. Products and/or services offered as well as the normal hours of operation;

21. Client base (list of clients with the percentage of sales each represents, market size, primary competitors, estimated market share and customer demographics);

22. List of all intangible assets such as any patents, trademarks, trade names, websites; email addresses, telephone numbers and copyrights.

Once this information was gathered, I began my "forensic" accounting process. I discussed the property value with the retail specialists in my office. At the heart of the discussion was the question, does being on the National Historic Registry make a property more valuable, and if it did, how much more valuable? To my surprise, the consensus was that being on the National Historic Registry could be a detriment as well as a blessing because of the restrictions that may be placed on the property in order to maintain that designation. In essence, there was no <u>added</u> value for being on the Historic Registry because the financial data already reflected that designation's effects (if any).

I then reviewed the sale prices of properties that had recently sold in other historic districts in her state at the time and found that most of those buildings were sold at multiples between $95.00 and $150.00 per square foot. I asked Rachael to supply me with some comparable sales in <u>her</u> resort area and they showed a similar multiple range of $75.00 to $135.00 per square foot. The subject building was 3,300 square feet in size and situated on a 5,000 square foot lot. If I applied the high end of the multiple range ($135.00 per square foot), the value of the real estate would be nearly $450,000. Using a mid-range multiple of $105.00 per square foot, the value came out to $347,000, which I intended to use in my report. Having established a target range of value for the real estate, I next turned my attention to the value of the retail business.

Small businesses are generally valued at a multiple of 2.0 to 3.0 times cash flow…but what exactly is this mysterious entity called *cash flow*? Apart from my earlier simplistic definition of cash flow, most business appraisers define cash flow as the Earnings of a business Before Interest, Depreciation, Taxes and Amortization (EBIDTA) are expensed. In my compilation of the cash flow, I included all owner compensation, i.e. wages, personal insurance, pension plan and other benefits, because in a small business the owner's compensation can really skew the net profit depending on how well the owner "treats" himself or herself. For example, the more an owner takes out of his or her business in salary and other compensation, the lower the net profit of the business.

Note: The only *interest* expense that should not be included in the cash flow is *floor plan interest*; i.e., the carrying cost that manufacturers charge their dealers for large ticket items such as motor vehicles, campers and major appliances. It is assumed that the purchaser of those types of businesses would continue to incur this expense after the sale.

Like many business owners who own rather than lease their premises, this property owner did not have an *arms-length* lease agreement and therefore was not charging her business any rent. When trying to determine the cash flow of any business, *a premises cost*, i.e., mortgage interest payments or rent, must obviously be included in the operating expenses. If the building's value is estimated to be $347,000 (certainly not more than $450,000), a fair market rent can often be calculated using ten percent of the building's value (a standard percentage commercial real estate agents use in establishing a fair market rent). This method identified a fair market rent of about

$35,000 per year with a top-end of $45,000 (approximately $3,000 to $3,700 per month). The boutique seller agreed to an annual rent figure of $40,000 ($3,333 per month) and was ready to have her attorney prepare a lease based on that amount.

The boutique had a net profit of $39,000, depreciation of $6,000, interest of $14,000, and an owner's compensation package of $55,000, for a total *provable* cash flow of $114,000. When the fair market rent of $40,000 was deducted, the cash flow dropped to $74,000.

Net Profit	$39,000
Depreciation	6,000
Interest	14,000
Compensation	55,000
Unadjusted Cash Flow	$114,000
Less Rent	- 40,000
Adjusted Cash Flow	$74,000

Because the boutique's sales had been slipping over the past three years, I felt a cash flow multiple of 2.4 would be appropriate (this multiple was totally subjective on my part), giving the business a value of about $178,000 (including all of its assets). When the estimated value of the business ($178,000) was added to the estimated value of the real estate ($347,000) the result was a total transaction value of about $525,000 - less than half of the $1.2 million requested by the seller.

Note: This is not meant to demean the seller or the seller's intentions because the seller had never requested a professional evaluation in order to set her asking price.

If Rachael had paid the $1.2 million asking price, which would have required an equity investment (down payment) of more than $250,000, the resulting debt service would have destroyed her financially (assuming a financial entity or the seller would have funded the acquisition in the first place). From the seller's standpoint, any default on the part of the buyer would force the seller to either sue the buyer for specific performance or take back the business and try to resurrect it. When Rachael reviewed my evaluation, she was extremely disappointed, but nonetheless, happy she hadn't made what could have been the biggest mistake of her life. She followed what has always been my mantra in business: **it is far better to do things right, than fast!**

Contrary to those who cite "rules of thumb" as a basis for valuing a business, I have found that most are not defensible. Those based solely on a multiple of net profit are highly questionable because they can be easily *gerrymandered*, i.e., as mentioned earlier, the net profit of any business can be *adjusted* either upward or downward depending on the amount of the owner's compensation. For example, a business showing a net profit of $50,000 and owner's compensation of $100,000 can be altered to show a net profit of $100,000 if the owner chooses to receive only $50,000 as annual compensation. This is the best example of why, in the evaluation of a small business, all of the owner's compensation must be factored into the cash flow.

The same is true of "rules of thumb" that cite multiples of gross sales. Businesses with identical gross sales can have vastly different cash flows depending on the operating expenses of each business. In fact, I have witnessed two identical fast-food franchises, serving the same product mix and market that had vastly different cash flows due to the individual franchisee's compensation package.

The acid test should be whether or not the cash flow of the business can service (retire) the debt (often in the form of a seller-held promissory note), pay the owner a suitable living wage and provide a reasonable return on the owner's initial investment (down payment). **If the business's cash flow does not satisfy those three important requirements, the deal should not be consummated.**

The previous example is a relatively simplistic overview of the evaluation process without showing the actual work that goes into the development of a defensible evaluation. On the following page is a more detailed explanation of the forensic accounting process featuring a fictional profit and loss statement. Much of the remainder of this chapter will focus on the expense categories and numbers shown in the following ABC, Inc. P&L.

ABC, INC. P&L

Gross Sales	$600,000
Cost of Sales	<u>300,000</u>
Gross Profit	300,000
Operating Expenses	
-Advertising	10,000
-Amortization	5,000
-Auto	7,000
-Depreciation	15,000
-Insurance	7,000
-Interest	10,000
-Maintenance	6,000
-Owner's salary	40,000
-Payroll	75,000
-Payroll taxes	15,000
-Professional fees	5,000
-Profit sharing	30,000
-Rent	45,000
-Telephone	8,000
-Travel/entertainment	5,000
-Utilities	<u>7,000</u>
Total Expenses	$290,000
Net Profit	**$14,000**

Following are components of a defensible cash flow as described in the previous pages.

	Add Back:	
	-Amortization	5,000
	-Depreciation	15,000
	-Interest	10,000
	-Owner's salary	40,000
	-Personal leased auto	7,000
	-Personal insurance	3,000
	-Personal travel	3,000
	-Owner's profit sharing	10,000
	Total Add-backs:	$93,000
	TOTAL CASH FLOW:	**$107,000**

ABC, Inc. has a net profit of $14,000 on sales of $600,000. Included in the annual operating expenses are: amortization ($5,000), depreciation ($15,000), interest ($10,000), owner's salary ($40,000), the owner's leased company car ($7,000), the owner's health insurance premium ($3,000), the owner's personal travel ($3,000), and the owner's portion of profit sharing ($10,000). When added together, the cash flow of this business is a respectable $107,000…which is a far more accurate depiction of its financial performance than just the $14,000 net profit figure. Based on the above data, this business would be worth between $214,000 (using a 2.0 multiple) and $321,000 (using a 3.0 multiple). Applying an average multiple of 2.5, the business is worth about $270,000. In order to more closely define the cash flow multiple, the following factors must be addressed:

1. **Business Age and History** - A well-established business generally commands a higher multiple than one less than three-years-old. This is especially true of a business that enjoys a good reputation and has suffered no damaging litigation nor has any potentially damaging litigation pending.

2. **Revenues** – Obviously growing sales make a business more valuable than one that is just keeping pace with inflation or experiencing shrinking sales.

3. **Employees** - Long-term, skilled and self-motivated employees create a higher multiple, as do key management people who remain on board after the sale. It is also important that employees are being paid a fair wage when compared to the existing labor market.

4. **Equipment** - Up-to-date and well-maintained equipment will often enable a business to command a higher multiple, especially if the equipment will support future growth. Leased equipment doesn't justify a higher multiple (all leased equipment should be identified as such on the equipment list).

5. **Real Estate** - If the business premises are leased, a long-term lease (involving both a fixed term and renewal options), at a fair market rent, is the ideal situation. If the real estate is being sold with the business, it should be priced at or below fair market value to command a higher multiple. A buyer will also want an environmental assessment (phase 1 study) for further peace of mind. Environmental problems can not only lower the multiple but may also be deal killers.

6. **Complexity** - A business that is easy-to-learn is generally more valuable than one requiring technical training. If a special license is required, e.g., general contractor, plumber, electrician, the buyer should be allowed to work under the seller's license until the buyer can qualify for one. The seller should always be willing to provide the training necessary to assure the continued success of the business. Any breech of these standard conditions will lower the multiple.

7. **Customer Base** - A growing and diverse customer base is very important and creates a higher multiple for the

business. Conversely, a business that depends on only a few large customers will seldom garner a multiple above 2.5. Other demographic information should also be considered such as the age and income per household within the existing market area.

8. **Magnitude of cash flow** - If the cash flow is less than $50,000, it can't provide much of a living wage for the buyer's family or service much debt, whereas a cash flow above $100,000 is far more desirable and tends to push the multiple higher.

It is important to note that the cash flow multiple can be increased even beyond 3.0 if one or more of the following conditions exist:

a) **The cash flow exceeds $200,000, and even more when it passes $300,000 and $500,000.** This is because those higher cash flows can service a great deal more debt and still provide the buyer with an attractive living wage. In these instances, the cash flow multiple can range from 3.0 to as much as 4.0.

b) **There are contracts in place that guarantee a steady revenue stream well into the future.** The best example of this is an insurance agency I sold that had a solid client base, and even if no other new clients were added, it would support the agency if the owner simply serviced the existing accounts. As in the above example, strong contractual relationships can also yield a multiple as high as 4.0.

c) **The business's rate of growth is stellar with no foreseeable slowdown.** Trying to value a "shooting star" is extremely difficult because there is no guarantee that the current rate of growth is sustainable. However, if it appears the business will be able to keep its trajectory for the next couple of years, it may warrant a multiple higher than 3.0.

d) **The company has new products or services in the pipeline that will likely generate additional future cash flow**. Nobody can predict the eventual success or failure of a new product or service, but if they are closely related to the company's proven offerings, the odds are in favor of customer acceptance.

e) **The existing management team will remain in place after the sale**. This most often occurs in the sale of larger businesses that are gobbled up in a merger. The acquiring entity will often pay more in order to maintain the status quo by not having to replace key personnel. It makes for a more seamless transaction and also eliminates a competitor.

The key to every business evaluation is being able to determine the true cash flow. A seller must be able to prove all the cash flow components, i.e., any expense that the seller claims is not business-related or is personal compensation must have a receipt or other validating document supporting the claim. Tax returns are always considered an essential part of this documentation process because they are signed under penalty of perjury.

When reviewing a business's tax returns or P&Ls, it is of paramount importance to realize that there are some accounting issues that can greatly impact the true cash flow calculation:

1. In some instances, such as in the first example where the owner of the business also owns the real estate, the tax return and/or P&L may not show a rental expense. In these situations, it is important to find out what a fair market rent would be for the property and include that expense as a negative add-back in the cash flow calculation.

2. If ma and pa are both working in the business and are included in the owner's or officer's compensation expense, an allowance must be made to cover the cost of replacing one of the two spouses. This approach assumes that most buyers are flying solo and that the subject business has required the

production of both spouses. The cost of replacing either ma or pa also becomes a negative add-back.

3. In the case of a Sole Proprietorship, the owner may take his or her salary in the form of a ***draw***. This term refers to the owner taking money out of the net profits of the business at certain intervals. A ***draw*** does not show up as the owner's compensation on the P&L. There is a tendency for an owner to want to include the ***draw*** in determining cash flow but that would be a huge mistake because a ***draw*** actually comes out of the net profit of the business and is not a part of the overall P&L expenses. If this is confusing, consider ABC, Inc. If this was a sole Proprietor instead of a Corporation, the owner could choose to take the *owner's salary* as a draw. This would eliminate the $40,000 salary as an expense and subsequently increase the net profit by the same amount, bringing it up to $54,000 - which would yield the same cash flow when combined with the "add-backs."

4. Another thing to be aware of is the subject of "Other Income" that sometimes shows up on tax returns. If the Other Income is recurring, such as rebates that are earned every year as a result of sales volume with a specific vendor, it can be counted as part of the *cash flow*. However, as is often the case, if the Other Income is derived from the sale of an asset or some other non-recurring source, it may not be included in the cash flow calculation.

5. Unlike S-Corporations, Limited Liability Companies and Sole Proprietorships, owners of C-Corporations may choose to use a fiscal year other than the typical calendar year interval for preparation of tax returns. This is an important distinction when reviewing tax return information especially during due diligence.

6. Finally, there are situations where the owner's compensation is not listed separately on the P&L or tax return but is included in the overall payroll expense. In these instances, a review of the owner's year-end W-2 form will provide the amount that

can be listed as an add-back.

There is a sanity test to employ when trying to decide if a business is fairly priced. As previously referenced on page 24, after a typical down payment (30% to 35%), the business's cash flow should be able to retire the balance of the debt and provide the buyer an adequate living wage. In the previous example (ABC, Inc.), if the buyer put down $90,000 (one-third) on an offer of $270,000, the debt service would be a little more than $2,700 per month $32,000 per year), on a seven year payout, at 7% annual interest (typical sale terms, circa 2014). Given a cash flow of $107,000, after servicing the $32,000 annual debt, the buyer would still have about $75,000 remaining that may be used as personal compensation, to fund an operating account reserve, and provide a return on investment (the down payment). This deal makes good financial sense.

Most cash flow evaluations assume a "turnkey" sale, which includes all of the tangible and intangible assets of the business: inventory, trade name, trademarks, patents, web site(s), telephone numbers, existing beneficial contracts, franchise (if applicable), furniture, fixtures and equipment. Simply stated, all the necessary components that make the business successful are in place at time of closing.

In retail businesses with large inventories, it often happens that the cash flow method of evaluation produces a value less than the asset value of the business. For example, say the cash flow of ABC, Inc. is $107,000 and the company has an inventory (at the company's cost) of about $200,000 along with an estimated value of $75,000 for all its other tangible assets. As previously mentioned, the $107,000 cash flow would yield an estimated value of $270,000 if an average multiple of 2.5 is used. That *cash flow generated value* is less than the estimated asset value, which means some adjustment needs to take place for the evaluation to make sense to a seller.

It is common for retail stores to stock more inventory than is economically feasible or practical, which often forces a costly year-end inventory reduction sale. With a little research, it is possible to determine what a "normal" level of inventory should exist to support a store's sales. In the above example, it was discovered that a normal inventory level of $100,000 was optimal for that type of retail operation. The *cash flow value* of the business, $270,000 (including $100,000 in inventory and $75,000 in tangible assets) now makes sense because it shows about $95,000 in **goodwill** which is the difference between the cash flow generated value of the business and the current value of its assets.

But what happens to the excess $100,000 in inventory? In some cases, the seller allows the buyer to sell the excess inventory on consignment, with the seller reimbursed for the cost of the excess inventory as it is sold. In other instances, the seller holds an inventory reduction sale prior to the consummation of the business sale. I always recommend that the buyer opt for the first scenario which puts the buyer in control of any inventory reduction because a pre-closing inventory liquidation sale can decrease normal customer traffic for several weeks following the closing...which is never a good situation for a new owner.

Here are some frequently asked questions regarding business evaluations:

What role does "potential" play in an evaluation? Sellers often point to *potential* in the evaluation process as rationale for convincing the broker to increase the value. Most experienced brokers explain to sellers, that buyers don't pay extra for the *potential* when acquiring a business because they believe that any *potential* they realize after the sale will be due to their time, hard work and investment. Realistically, a buyer won't purchase a business unless it has at least some potential - but also won't pay extra for any pre-sale potential the business exhibits.

Should "projections" be used in the evaluation process? Because all projections are totally subjective, using them to determine the value of future cash flow can be dangerous and possibly lead to a lawsuit if a buyer feels there was any misrepresentation. A seller may feel the projected cash flow is attainable but the buyer may not possess the same work ethic or business acumen, thereby making those projections unattainable for the buyer. If a buyer bases an acquisition decision on a value determined by projected cash flow, there is a danger of overpaying which could result in the buyer's inability to service the debt.

When evaluating businesses, I choose to rely only upon historic and provable financial data with a focus on the most current three years. Attempting to predict future sales and earnings in today's volatile economy is like trying to pick the winning number on a roulette wheel. Just ask those who lost their shirts in the real estate crash of 2008.

Can "tax issues" affect an evaluation? Prior to consummating a transaction, chattel and tax lien searches are conducted to determine if there are any impediments standing in the way of a closing. If the tax lien search shows there are back taxes due, the buyer will likely deduct the unpaid taxes from the cash flow for the years in which the taxes were left unpaid. The assumption is that the buyer will pay all the state and federal taxes when they come due. In this scenario, the buyer may feel it necessary to re-evaluate the entire business before the closing can take place.

If the Chattel search shows that money is still owed on some of the tangible assets, the value of those assets may be adjusted downward proportionately by the buyer and a re-evaluation of the business may be requested.

CHAPTER THREE:

CASH VS. TERMS

One of the more difficult decisions a seller has to make is whether or not to finance the business sale. This is a legitimate concern because it centers around the seller's greatest fear: not receiving full payment following the sale of the business. It is therefore highly important to examine all of the factors that a seller needs to address prior to making this critical decision.

1. *RISK. There is no argument to the fact that a cash sale eliminates any risk to a seller...so let's stipulate to that fact right up front. However, it is important to examine the other key factors before deciding on a financing strategy.*

2. *PRICE. A buyer who pays all-cash for a business expects to receive an offsetting discount in the purchase price, often as much as fifteen to twenty percent. To a seller looking to the sale of a business as a means of funding a comfortable retirement, every dollar is important, so a discounted purchase price is not a very attractive option. Sellers can maximize the value/price of their businesses by financing the transaction.*

3. *MARKETABILITY. It's a simple fact that buyers want sellers to "have some skin in the game." In other words, they want the seller participating in some of the risks associated with the ownership transition. A seller's refusal to fund some portion of the sale sends a warning signal to a buyer that maybe the seller is hiding something or is not very optimistic about the buyer's chances for future success. It has been my experience that a cash-only sale requirement eliminates as many as*

85% of potential buyers.

4. **LISTING TERM.** Due to the difficulty in marketing a cash-only sale, many business brokers require a longer listing term...often as long as a year or more, whereas listings that allow for some seller-financing generally command only a six-month listing term.

5. **TAX TREATMENT.** Most accountants will agree that a seller-financed installment sale will ultimately save the seller some taxes when compared to a lump-sum cash sale. I suggest that sellers confirm this statement with their respective accountants.

6. **INTEREST RETURN.** Most seller-financed transactions command an interest rate of six to eight percent on the promissory note (circa 2014). Compare that to what you might receive with a bank certificate of deposit, stock dividend, or money market account. The higher interest rate should offset at least some of the risk of seller financing.

7. **TIME REQUIRED TO CLOSE.** Most cash transactions rely on some combination of SBA and bank financing, which can take as long as two or more months to acquire (not to mention the mountain of red tape that will have to be scaled). A seller-financed sale can be closed in less than a month, and in fact, I have closed some in only a week. Every day that passes between the executed purchase agreement and the closing can bring both unnecessary and unanticipated problems. If speed is of the essence, a cash-only transaction isn't a realistic option.

8. **MITIGATING FACTORS.** As in any *proven* process, there are mitigating factors that can make a cash-only sale the only alternative. For example, cash (or mostly cash) may be necessary if:

    a) The seller needs to pay off a significant amount of

debt to clear the business's assets from any liens, debts or other encumbrances that may impede or even prevent the closing. In these instances, any debts are paid off from the proceeds of the sale immediately after closing.

b) The seller needs a large down payment in order to purchase another business or make some other capital investment.

c) The seller is sick or elderly, with a limited amount of time left, and needs to put his or her affairs in order to avoid probate. An 80-year-old seller seldom wants to carry a seven-year note.

9. **IN THE EVENT OF DEFAULT.** Because the seller's promissory note contains the buyer's <u>personal guarantee</u>, the seller can look to the buyer's personal assets for repayment. The way this process works is: the buyer is notified in writing, by either the seller or the seller's attorney, about the late payment, and is put on notice, that if payment is not received by a specific date as outlined in the promissory note, the entire sum will immediately become due and payable. If payment is still not received, the seller has the right to petition the court for a default judgment. When (if) the judgment is granted, the seller may sell off the assets of the business for whatever price they bring and then pursue the buyer's personal assets for any outstanding balance, OR take back the business and resume its operation.

In the event of a default judgment, all of the buyer's personal assets are at risk with the exception of retirement accounts and a portion of the buyer's home equity. Ask your attorney for further clarification of the default judgment laws in your state.

The risk to the seller in carrying a note can be lessened if the seller views *due diligence* much the same as a buyer. The seller should review the buyer's financial statement and credit report with the same scrutiny that a bank applies to loan applications. The three most important considerations for the seller are:

1. The size of the buyer's down payment (a minimum of 25% of the purchase price);

2. The buyer's credit report (a minimum score of 650); and

3. The buyer's financial statement (showing assets sufficient to satisfy the terms of the promissory note in the event of default).

If any one of these three components is weak, the other two must be very strong AND the seller should still use extreme caution. If two of the three components are weak, the seller should walk away from the deal. If the buyer has sufficient financial resources and a sterling credit report, a seller-financed deal might be in the best interests of both parties.

CHAPTER FOUR:

SELECTING THE RIGHT BUSINESS BROKER

When the time comes to buy or sell a business, one of the most crucial decisions will be the choice of a broker to assist you in the process. Here are some guidelines to help you select the broker who will best serve your needs.

1. **Interview candidates**. Call your attorney, accountant, banker or business associates for referrals or simply search the Yellow Pages for the names of business brokers serving your area. Set up a meeting with at least two business brokers and interview them the same way you would interview a potential employee. Pay special attention to whether the candidates are more concerned with your needs or simply earning a commission.

2. **Experience counts**. The sale or purchase of a business can be extremely complex, requiring creative approaches to unique problems. An experienced broker understands the emotional, financial and practical issues involved and can resolve problems with time-tested solutions. Ask how long each candidate has been in business, how many transactions they have handled (especially businesses similar to yours), and if they specialize in business sales. Don't fall prey to a commercial or residential real estate agent who claims to have "sold a few businesses" in the past. Because of the potentially litigious nature of business brokerage, any errors or omissions on the part of the broker can end up creating unnecessary and unwanted courtroom drama. Most business professionals understand and appreciate the need for specialization.

3. **Demand honesty**. Beware of the broker who only tells you what you want to hear! If your sales are faltering or if you have been "skimming" from your business, an honest

broker will suggest that you operate your business for at least another year in order to show the business in its true light, rather than take a quick listing at an indefensible price. The honest broker will only quote the list price when asked by a prospective buyer, "How low do you think the seller will go?" It takes an honest broker to tell you when your price and terms are out of sync with the market and give you concrete reasons to prove the point. An honest broker will show prospective buyers what they can afford to pay for a business and not take them down fantasy lane ending in impossible negotiations with frustrating results. For example, if a buyer has $50,000 as an equity investment (down payment), an astute business broker knows better than to show that person a million-dollar business.

4. **Expect pre-sale confidentiality**. Having your customers, employees, vendors and competitors know your business is for sale can be disastrous. Conversely, potential buyers don't want their current employers to know that they are considering a career change. The marketing and screening policies utilized by credible business brokers assure that only qualified prospects will receive proprietary information on a specific business opportunity and that all identities will be protected.

The easiest thing in the world is for a business broker to answer all of the questions that are posed by potential business buyers. However, if those questions deal with the name or address of a business, or any other identifying characteristics, prior to the signing of a Nondisclosure or Confidentiality Agreement, the broker is not honoring the seller's privacy. Don't be afraid to ask the prospective broker how those "easy" questions will be answered.

5. **Ask for references**. Any professional should be willing to provide the names of past clients as references. Don't accept the excuse that all sales information must be kept confidential. After a successful consummation of a sale,

most sellers and buyers have no problem with public disclosure of the transaction as long as the terms of the sale are not divulged. The only real "proof of broker performance" is through such disclosure, so don't let a broker hide behind the cloak of confidentiality. If a broker is telling you everything you want to hear, assume the same is occurring with the other party to the transaction.

6. **Local vs. national brokers**. Some sellers believe that the only way they can receive national exposure is by listing with a national company. If this was true in the past, it certainly is not true today. The Internet has become the great equalizer in business marketing, affording local companies the same global audience as brokerages with offices throughout the U.S.

People moving from other parts of the country seldom contact a national broker. Instead, they contact local chambers of commerce, bankers, Realtors, accountants, attorneys or personal acquaintances to acquire the information they seek. Through these contacts, they are often referred to a business broker best suited to handle their needs.

The primary advantage local brokerages have over national firms is a better knowledge of the local market, from zoning laws to licensing requirements, current economic news to local business customs. Hiring a broker who knows the "lay of the land" and is the beneficiary of local referrals can be very advantageous to both the buyer and seller. Another key difference between local and national brokers is the fact that many national companies charge up-front fees, ranging from a few thousand dollars to tens of thousands, to simply prepare expensive appraisal and marketing pieces. An additional fee is charged if the national company is able to sell the business. On the other hand, most local business brokers only get paid for results, i.e., if a sale doesn't occur, no commission is paid.

7. **Pay the piper**. Most local business brokers charge a commission of ten to twelve percent of the total sales price. In the case of a very small business sale, a minimum commission may also be required due to the vast amount of time and effort it takes to complete any transaction, whether it's $20,000 or $2,000,000. As is the case with most services, you generally get what you pay for, and an extra two percent can seem cheap when you are negotiating a complicated $500,000 sale with a 10-year lease, a seven-year promissory note, a five-year covenant not to compete, the transfer of patents or trademarks and a six-month training and consulting period.

8. **Make sure the broker is insured**. Business brokerage requires a very different kind of E&O (errors & omissions) insurance than commercial or residential real estate sales. Ask the prospective broker for proof of insurance before you put your fate in his/her hands.

CHAPTER FIVE:

UNDERSTANDING THE LISTING AGREEMENT

Once the seller's team is in place and a pricing and marketing strategy have been agreed to, the next step is to enter into a Listing Agreement in order to authorize the business broker to begin marketing the business. There are three versions of a Listing Agreement that you should be aware of:

1. **Sole and Exclusive Right to Sell Listing**. This type of listing is the most broker-friendly because it guarantees the broker a commission no matter who sells the business.

Pros and Cons: While the Sole and Exclusive Listing is the most broker-friendly, it also assures the seller that there is a responsible party marketing the business. A broker will work harder under this type of an agreement because the seller has shown good faith in hiring the broker under these conditions. An earned commission can be cheap compensation if a suitable sale is negotiated with the help of a professional.

2. **Exclusive Agency Listing**. This listing form guarantees the broker a commission in the event the broker sells the business but it does not exclude the business owner from selling the business through his/her own efforts.

Pros and Cons: A competent professional will generally refuse to work under this type of listing because it is too easy for a buyer, introduced to the business by the broker, to go behind the broker's back and cut a deal with the seller by using a "straw buyer" (a friend or relative who takes the original buyer's role in the transaction in order to save a commission). A seller trying to act as his or her own business broker is similar to a defendant in a jury trial attempting to be his or her own lawyer.

3. **Open Listing**. This type of listing allows every broker to attempt to sell the business, with a commission due only to the selling broker. However, as in the previous example, the seller may also sell the business and pay no commission.

Pros and Cons: An Open Listing is extremely dangerous for a seller because there is no responsible party disseminating factual information. If an incompetent, unscrupulous or untrained broker gives out incorrect information about the business, the seller (along with the broker) may be sued for misrepresentation if the deal goes sour.

The following chapter shows a standard Listing Agreement that I have used for my more than thirty years. In order to help you understand the Agreement, here is an explanation of its primary components:

Section A. This section lists general information about the business, such as its name (ABC, Inc.), address and ownership. Lines 1 through 3 are self-explanatory.

Line 4 (Seller/Owner) asks for the business's legal entity name, i.e., corporation (ABC, Inc.), limited liability company (ABC, LLC) or partnership (ABC, Ltd.), and not the name of the president or managing partner. The only time a person's name should be on this line is if the legal entity is the name of the owner, e.g., John Smith, Inc., or if the legal entity is a sole proprietor.

Line 5 shows the type of legal entity, i.e., C-Corporation, S-Corporation, Limited Liability Company, Partnership, Limited Partnership or Sole Proprietor.

Line 6 lists the person to contact who will act as the spokesperson for the business and be the source of future information.

Line 7 shows the latest full year's financial performance in terms of annual sales and resulting cash flow. It is the seller's responsibility to be able to prove whatever figures are listed on this line because that will be the financial information that the business broker will provide to a potential buyer.

Section B. This important section lists the Proposed Terms of Sale which will be presented to potential buyers by the broker.

Line 1, the purchase price, needs to be expressed both in writing and numerically. The broker's fee is also shown on this line as being included in the purchase price. Some states impose a gross receipts tax on the brokerage commission, but if your state does not have such a tax, the reference to "plus tax" can be eliminated.

Line 2 states the down payment the seller is willing to accept (which includes the broker's commission) to be paid at closing.

Line 3 outlines the terms of the seller's note and specifies that the note is secured by both the business's assets and the buyer's personal guarantee. At this time (circa 2014), the standard interest rate runs between six and eight percent and the note term between five and ten years.

Line 4 shows the total list price that will be presented to prospective buyers. By law,
this is the only price a broker is allowed to quote when asked, "How much do you think the seller will take for the business?"

Line 5 lists the value of the inventory that will be included in the total purchase price and conveyed to the buyer at closing. This is the seller's best estimate of the inventory level needed to sustain future business operations following the closing. In most cases the buyer and seller will count the inventory prior to the closing and sometimes with the aid of an inventory counting service (when there is a large amount of inventory to be counted). At the time the inventory is taken, if it exceeds the amount allocated in the Purchase Agreement, the seller has the right to ask the buyer for the overage, usually as an add-on to the promissory note. However, if the actual inventory is less than the allocated value, the buyer can ask that the purchase price be discounted by that amount.

Section C. This paragraph is reserved for any other terms and/or conditions that are not part of the standard listing agreement.

Section D. The relationship between the seller and broker is expressed in the next few paragraphs. It is important that the name of the business brokerage firm, and not the individual broker, is listed on the appropriate line. The same is true for the actual legal entity in the "seller" space.

Paragraph #1 shows that the Listing Agreement is Sole and Exclusive, which means, as previously stated, that no matter who sells the business, the broker will receive a commission. It is this provision that also charges the broker with the sole responsibility to do everything within the broker's power to secure a ready, willing and able buyer within the time frame that is specified in this paragraph.

Paragraph #2 confirms the broker's acceptance of the responsibilities as outlined in the Listing Agreement and the broker's commitment to providing the best possible services in a confidential manner.

Paragraph #3 states the commission that the seller will pay to the broker following a successful closing or if the seller arbitrarily decides to take the business off the market or negate a sale after a contract is signed. This section also protects the broker by providing an eighteen month window, following the expiration of the Listing Agreement, during which a commission will be due the broker in the event the seller negotiates a sale with a party introduced to the seller by the broker prior to the listing's expiration.

Paragraph #4 assures the buyer that the business will remain intact and as represented until closing and that it is in compliance with all federal, state and local rules and regulations.

Paragraph #5 outlines the assurances (warranties) the seller is willing to make to both the buyer and broker as part of the transaction, the seller's commitment to stand behind those assurances, and the venue in which any breach of those assurances would be adjudicated.

Paragraph #6 discusses what will happen to the earnest money if the buyer backs out of the transaction after due diligence. The seller and broker will divide any earnest money deposit after any legal or collection expenses are paid.

Paragraph #7 restates the broker's commitment to market the business to the best of the broker's ability but no guarantee of sale is made.

Paragraph #8 defines the process for any possible litigation arising after the Listing
Agreement is signed, whether the litigation involves the broker, buyer or seller. By stipulating that the loser pays the winner's attorney's fees and court costs, this provision discourages any frivolous lawsuits. The remainder of the document provides space for the seller's and broker's signatures.

CHAPTER SIX:

SOLE AND EXCLUSIVE LISTING AGREEMENT

A. BUSINESS INFORMATION

   1. Business Name:
_____

   2. Business Address:
_____

   3. Type of Business:
_____

   4. Seller/Owner:
_____

   5. Form of Ownership:
_____

   6. Person to Contact: _____ Phone: (___)_____

   7. 20___ Annual Sales - $_____.00   20___ Cash Flow - $_____.00

B. PROPOSED TERMS OF SALE

   1. Purchase Price of _____ Thousand and No/100 Dollars ($_____.00) including Broker's fee of $_____.00 (plus tax) to be paid as follows:

   2. $_____.00 Cash Down Payment (includes $_____.00 Broker's fee (plus tax) paid at closing, through escrow, or at possession of the business by PURCHASER, whichever occurs first.

3. $_____.00   Note to SELLER, to be secured by both the Business's assets and the Purchaser's personal guarantee, and to be paid as follows: $_____ or more per month, for ___ months, including ___% annual interest.

4. $_____.00   TOTAL PURCHASE PRICE

5. Estimated Inventory of $_____.00, valued at Seller's cost, to be included in   the total purchase price (the purchase price will be adjusted by any variance).

C. ADDITIONAL REMARKS

_____

_____

D. TERMS AND PROVISIONS OF LISTING

In consideration of the actual promises set forth below, _____ (BROKER) and _____ (SELLER) contract as follows:

    1. SELLER hereby employs BROKER and gives BROKER the SOLE AND EXCLUSIVE RIGHT to sell or otherwise convey all or any part of that Business described above, on the Proposed Terms set forth above, or for any other price and terms to which SELLER may agree, and this employment will continue in effect, and cannot be terminated or canceled without the written consent of both SELLER and BROKER, until 12:00 midnight, _____, 20___, and will automatically terminate at that time.

    2. BROKER hereby accepts employment and promises to use its best efforts, in BROKER'S ordinary course of business, and in a confidential manner, to offer for sale and to procure a ready, willing and able purchaser for the Business described above. SELLER hereby appoints BROKER as the sole and exclusive agent and authorizes BROKER to present any and all offers BROKER may

receive, until such time as SELLER accepts an Offer to Purchase, presented by BROKER on behalf of a purchaser, at which time BROKER need not advise SELLER of any subsequent offer(s) received for the Business until after forfeiture by the purchaser or other nullification of the purchase contract. Additionally, BROKER is authorized to accept deposits and issue receipts for deposit on such offers. SELLER grants to BROKER the right to advertise and show the Business at times that are agreeable to SELLER.

3. SELLER agrees to pay BROKER a fee in an amount equal to ____% of the Total Purchase Price, plus the appropriate tax (if applicable), immediately if any of the following occur:

a) BROKER procures a purchaser, ready, willing and able to purchase the Business on the Proposed Terms herein; or

b) SELLER sells, leases or otherwise conveys all or any part of the Business during the Sole and Exclusive Period, regardless of whether or not BROKER was involved in or responsible for such disposition; or SELLER enters into a sale contract, accepts a deposit, opens an escrow or records a notice of intention to sell the Business; or

c) SELLER withdraws the Business from sale, or purports to terminate this listing contract prior to the expiration of the Sole and Exclusive Period; or

d) SELLER fails or refuses to complete a sale or the conveyance of all or any part of the Business after entering into a written agreement to do so; or

e) SELLER sells, leases or otherwise conveys all or any part of the Business within eighteen (18) months from the termination date of the Sole and Exclusive Period, to any person, firm or entity referred to the Business through the efforts of BROKER during the Sole and Exclusive Period. BROKER agrees to send SELLER a list of all parties introduced to SELLER'S business within 30 days following expiration of this agreement.

4. SELLER represents and warrants that SELLER (and the Business operation as applicable) is now, and shall remain, in full compliance with all local, state, and federal laws, rules and regulations regarding the operations and sale of the Business described above. To the best of SELLER'S knowledge, the leasehold for the business herein named is in full compliance with all federal, state and municipal environmental laws, rules, ordinances, regulations and requirements; and there has not been a spill or discharge of any hazardous substances or hazardous waste on those premises.

5. SELLER understands and hereby acknowledges that all facts, figures and other information set forth above, and all additional supporting documentation pertaining to the Business have been provided to BROKER by SELLER, and BROKER will rely upon SELLER'S representations of such facts, figures and other information when describing and promoting the Business to potential purchasers, without making any investigation into the accuracy of such representations by SELLER. Therefore, SELLER hereby represents and warrants that all such facts, figures and other information set forth above are true and accurate. SELLER hereby indemnifies and holds harmless BROKER against any and all claims, demands, causes for action, losses, fees and fees on appeals arising out of a breach of this warranty, and further agrees the county in which BROKER'S office is located is proper venue for any such action or suit in connection with any omissions or misrepresentations made by or on behalf of SELLER relative to the Business [SELLER (or SELLER'S representatives if applicable) to initial here ____].

6. As agent for SELLER, BROKER, or any other authorized escrow agent, is hereby authorized to accept, receipt for, and hold all money paid or deposited as a binder thereon in accordance with the law, and if such deposit is forfeited by the prospective purchaser, BROKER may retain one-half of such deposit, after any legal and collection expenses are paid, but not exceeding the total amount of BROKER'S compensation as described in paragraph #3 of this Agreement.

7. SELLER understands that by this Agreement BROKER does not guarantee the sale of the above Business, but that BROKER will make an earnest and continued effort to sell same until this Agreement is terminated.

8. LITIGATION. SELLER and BROKER agree, that in the event any litigation is instituted to collect any sum due BROKER, to enforce or interpret any of the provisions of this Agreement, or for any other reasons, the prevailing party or parties shall be entitled to recover from the other(s) their reasonable attorney's fees and court costs, including appeals, as determined by the Court in such action or suit.

THIS IS A LEGALLY BINDING CONTRACT. PLEASE READ IT CAREFULLY BEFORE SIGNING.

By signing this Agreement, SELLER (or SELLER'S representative, as applicable) hereby acknowledges having read and approved the attached Marketing Package, and authorizes BROKER to distribute the Marketing Package to potential buyers.

I/We, as SELLER (or SELLER'S representative, as applicable) have read, understand, and hereby agree to the above terms and provisions of this Agreement and any addendum hereto, and hereby acknowledge receipt of a copy of this Agreement.

Also, I/we represent and warrant that in entering into this Agreement, I/we act on behalf of SELLER, and all of the owners, partners, shareholders of SELLER, and the business listed herein, and personally guarantee performance of this Agreement and are duly authorized to enter into this Agreement on behalf of SELLER and the Business.

Dated: _____, 20___ at: _____a.m. _____p.m.

Seller:_____(Legal Entity)_____

By: _____(Signature)_____
              (title)

                                          _____
                                                    Transaction Broker

CHAPTER SEVEN:

THE NONDISCLOSURE AGREEMENT

It will be your broker's responsibility to market your business and qualify prospective buyers by making sure they have the necessary resources, both financial and intellectual. Once that determination is made, the broker typically requires the potential buyer to sign a non-disclosure agreement (NDA) to ensure the seller's confidentiality through to the date of closing. Following is a standard NDA:

In connection with the possible acquisition (the "Proposed Transaction") by you (the "Buyer") of _____ (the "Business"), _____ (the "Seller") has furnished you information (the "Proprietary Information") regarding the Business. Buyer acknowledges that the Seller desires to maintain the Confidentiality of the Proprietary Information and agrees not to disclose or permit access to any Proprietary Information, without the prior written consent of Seller, to anyone other than Buyer's legal counsel, accountants, lenders or other agents or advisors to whom access or disclosure is necessary for Buyer to evaluate the Business.

Proprietary Information shall be defined as all information, including the fact that the Business is for sale, in any medium or format, which Buyer receives, either directly or indirectly from the Seller concerning the Business. This definition of Proprietary Information does not include any information that: (a) is readily available and known to the public; (b) is or becomes published on or after the date of disclosure to Buyer; (c) is in the Buyer's possession at the time of disclosure of such information to Buyer by Seller; (d) or is independently developed by the Buyer without reference to or reliance upon the information disclosed by the Seller.

In consideration of obtaining said Proprietary Information, Buyer agrees as follows:

1. All of the terms of this Agreement shall remain in effect for Three (3) years from the date hereon.

2. If Buyer decides not to pursue the Proposed Transaction, Buyer will promptly advise Seller of this fact and return to Seller all Proprietary Information furnished to Buyer without retaining copies, summaries, analyses or extracts thereof. Buyer agrees not to use the Proprietary Information to harm the Business by: (a) contacting its customers, employees, suppliers or landlords; (b) by lingering or otherwise observing the Business without Seller's consent; (c) or by starting a competing business within the existing market of the Business, <u>if Buyer is not currently doing business within this market.</u> Buyer agrees that it will use the Proprietary Information solely for the purposes of determining whether Buyer would be interested in pursuing a possible acquisition of all or part of the Business.

3. This Agreement shall be construed under and governed by the laws of the State of _____. The venue for any action instituted to enforce any terms of this Agreement shall be in the county in which the Business is located.

This Agreement may be signed in counterparts and faxed and electronic signatures will be considered as originals. If Buyer is a corporation, partnership, limited liability company or any other legal entity other than an Individual, the undersigned executes this Agreement on behalf of Buyer and warrants that he/she is duly authorized to do so.

Buyer acknowledges receipt of a fully executed copy of this Agreement.

Agreed to and accepted this ___th day of _____, 20___.

_____   _____
Name (Print)   Signature

Address: _____

_____   _____
   Telephone Number   Email Address

****

Once the NDA is signed, the broker generally offers the prospective buyer a marketing package that provides enough detail regarding the business's operations to whet the buyer's appetite, but only limited financial information (no tax returns, income statements or balance sheets). If the prospective buyer decides to pursue the acquisition to its next stage, the broker arranges a meeting with the seller wherein the two parties will be able to ask each other pertinent questions. Sometimes sellers prefer the initial meeting to be held in the broker's offices so that total confidentiality is assured. In other scenarios, the initial meeting takes place at the seller's place of business either before or after business hours. It is the seller's responsibility to decide upon the most comfortable scenario.

CHAPTER EIGHT:

THE SELLING PROCESS

The first step in the actual selling process or chronology is the discrete marketing of the business to ready, willing and able buyers. There are several national/global websites that business brokers use to market a business (circa 2014): www.BizBuySell.com, www.globalbx.com, www.brokerworks.com, www.businessbrokerages.com, www.mergerplace.com, and www.businessbroker.net. Most of these sites charge between $30.00 and $40.00 per month to list businesses and most potential business buyers look at two or more of these site in their search, so listing a business on all six sites really isn't necessary.

In order to maintain the confidentiality of the business, most of the information provided on the websites is fairly generic in nature, e.g., Manufacturing business in Seattle area with more than $1 million in sales and $300,000 cash flow. Some seller financing may be available for qualified buyer. For additional information, contact (email address and telephone number).

No other pertinent information is provided until the prospective buyer signs the Nondisclosure Agreement. Once the NDA is signed, a marketing package is presented to the prospective buyer that contains a great deal more information but not as proprietary as detailed profit and loss statements, tax returns or customer lists.

In order to retain a measure of confidentiality when providing a customer list, a seller will often label the customers as A, B, C, etc., along with a description of how much each customer contributes to the overall business's sales.

If, after reading the marketing package the prospect wishes to pursue the acquisition, a meeting is arranged by the broker to introduce the two parties and allow the prospect to ask for more intimate details surrounding the business. This meeting also provides the seller with an opportunity to ask pertinent questions about the prospective buyer's experience and qualifications and to determine the prospect's credit-worthiness. After this meeting, if both parties wish to proceed, the seller will usually grant the broker permission to release more detailed financial information, i.e., tax returns and financial statements, to help the buyer develop a business plan and structure an offer. However, if the seller leaves the meeting convinced the prospective buyer is incapable of running the business, negotiations can be quickly terminated by the business broker without any repercussions or hard feelings towards the owner.

Assuming the meeting the meeting proves satisfactory and the necessary information is conveyed to the prospective buyer, the business broker will then assist the prospective buyer in preparing an Offer to Purchase.

In the event the buyer requests seller financing, the purchase agreement should be accompanied by a copy of the buyer's financial statement and credit report so the seller and the seller's accountant can evaluate the buyer as a potential credit risk.

Sellers should <u>never</u> announce the pending sale to employees prior to closing. I have found that the perceived evil (new owner) is often far worse than the actual, and employees will tend to start searching for a new job if alerted to the fact that the business is for sale. After the closing, the seller can introduce a "real person" to the employees, followed by a pep talk from the buyer as to the company's future and each employee's role in that future.

Once the buyer completes due diligence, the Purchase Agreement is given to the neutral escrow attorney who transforms the abbreviated Purchase Agreement into the final, multi-page closing documents that encompass all the legalese necessary to make the buyer and seller feel comfortable, while allowing their respective attorneys to believe they have protected their clients to the best of their abilities.

CHAPTER NINE:

NEGOTIATING AN ASSET PURCHASE AGREEMENT

Most buyers are encouraged by their attorneys to purchase <u>only the assets</u> (asset sale) of a closely-held corporation rather than its corporate <u>stock</u> (stock sale) for fear of incurring contingent liabilities that may be lurking in the past and which could return to haunt a new owner. When a person buys the stock of a closely-held corporation, he or she is buying the history of that business, which could include a potential lawsuit resulting from an accident or some product failure incurred by the business in previous years.

The only time a stock sale makes sense is when there are valuable contracts in the name of the corporation that may take a great deal of time and effort to transfer to the buyer if done through an asset sale. In this event, the Stock Purchase Agreement should contain *sufficient indemnification and hold harmless* language for the buyer's protection. This is when an attorney's input becomes extremely valuable.

A stock sale generally provides better tax treatment for the seller, but because it comes at the expense of the buyer (the buyer must assume the seller's balance sheet with all of its depreciated assets), it usually results in a lower purchase price than does an asset sale. An experienced accountant can provide further rationale and explanation regarding the advantages and disadvantage of a stock sale. Practically speaking, however, out of more than 900 transactions that I have overseen, only a handful involved the purchase of corporate stock, so I will not be delving further into that subject in this book.

As previously mentioned, the Asset Purchase Agreement should include all of the tangible and intangible assets of the business that make the business run successfully:

> h)   all furniture, fixtures and equipment (in good working condition) required to operate the business;

i) a normal level of inventory and supplies valued at the seller's cost;

j) a leasehold interest that runs at least as long as the seller's promissory note
(SBA/bank-financed sales typically require a ten-year lease, which can consist of a fixed term plus renewal options);

k) a list of all customers, clients and vendors along with their addresses and other contact information (generally conveyed immediately after closing;

l) all company patents, trade names, trademarks, website addresses, telephone numbers, email addresses and business directory ads;

m) any existing franchise agreement, service contracts, equipment leases, Yellow Page contract, website hosting agreement or other beneficial contracts that will allow the buyer to maintain the successful operation of the business.

All of the tangible assets that are to be conveyed in the sale should be defined in an equipment list so that there is no question as to what the buyer can expect to receive. A complete list of both the tangible and intangible assets will be included in the Bill of Sale and used as collateral to guarantee payment on any promissory note.

Some sellers are reluctant to include the name of their businesses as one of the intangible assets because a business sale can be an emotional roller coaster. This can be disastrous to a buyer, because the trade name contains much of the "goodwill" associated with the business. Fortunately, most sellers understand this fact and agree to the name transfer. In those instances where the seller and buyer are unable to resolve this conflict, I suggest that the buyer be allowed to use the name through a transition period - often as long as three to five years. For example, if John Doe is selling his business to Amy Smith, during that transition period, the business name, *John Doe*

Enterprises, Inc. would remain the same for the first year. After that initial year, the name could segue to *John Doe - Amy Smith Enterprises, Inc.,* which in turn becomes *Amy Smith, Enterprises, Inc.*

When the seller of a business also owns the real property - according to my experience less than ten percent of the time - either the lease or purchase of the property should be part of any agreement. A lease is often in the best interests of both parties because it preserves the buyer's cash reserves while providing the seller with another source of income in addition to future appreciation in the property's value. By leasing, the seller also avoids a double tax hit. Buyers can protect their *future* interest in the property by asking the seller for a **first right of refusal** or an **option** to buy the property at a later date.

A first right of refusal allows the buyer to be first in line to purchase the property if or when the seller/landlord receives a bona fide offer from an interested third party. It is generally worded in the following manner:

> "In regard to the business property located at _____ (address)_____, in the event the owner receives a bona fide offer from a third party for the purchase of the business's premises, the buyer of the business known as (_____ business _____) has a *first right of refusal* to meet the terms of that offer, and in doing so, acquire the premises on those same conditions and terms. Buyer will have thirty (30) days, following the owner's written notification of the third party offer, to enter into a purchase agreement for said property. In the event buyer does not execute a purchase agreement within the thirty-day period, owner shall have the right to sell the property to the third party."

An option to purchase is different from a *first right of refusal* because it is executed at the same time as the buyer purchases the business and it stipulates a fixed future price and terms at that time, or at the very least, a formula whereby the business buyer and property owner can determine the future value of the property. One popular method is for each party to hire an appraiser and then attempt to have them achieve a meeting of the minds. If that doesn't work, a third appraiser is then hired as a mediator. An option to purchase is typically worded as follows:

> "Seller hereby grants to buyer an option to purchase the real estate located at (_____address_____) and identified as (__name of business__), on the following terms and conditions (__price and terms or formula__) until (__termination date__). In the event buyer does not purchase the subject real estate within that time period, seller may sell the real estate to a third party."

For a buyer, *all* of the assets, both tangible and intangible, that made the business a success are important...so any exclusion without a logical explanation could serve as a red flag and possibly kill the deal.

CHAPTER TEN:

UNDERSTANDING THE ASSET PURCHASE AGREEMENT

In addition to enumerating both the tangible and intangible assets being purchased, the Purchase Agreement should contain all of the terms and conditions that are necessary for the transaction to be fair and balanced. That doesn't guarantee that all of the buyer's desires will be realized, but it's a good platform from which to launch the attempted acquisition. It's important to note the sale price may not be the most important factor in negotiations - sometimes it is preempted by such factors as the size of the down payment or monthly payments, length of training and consulting, or the ability to obtain a suitable new lease or lease assignment.

Purchase Agreements generally contain a list of **contingencies**, i.e., issues that must be satisfied *before* closing, such as: (a) an inspection of books, records and equipment (due diligence); (b) acquisition of financing if the transaction is not being seller-financed; (c) negotiation of a suitable new lease or lease assignment; or (d) obtaining the approval of a franchisor or key vendor. All contingencies require a deadline for completion so they don't drag on indefinitely. In the event any contingency is not satisfied within the stated time frame, the transaction may be terminated and the buyer's earnest money refunded. It is important for the seller, whenever possible, to assist the buyer in satisfying these contingencies in a timely manner.

Purchase Agreements also include **conditions**, i.e., items that typically *follow* the closing, such as: (a) free training (the time frame depends on the complexity of the business and the relative experience of the buyer); (b) free consulting (primarily by telephone) that follows the initial training period; and (c) a non-compete agreement (typically for five years and limited to the business's existing market area).

The following pages contain an outline of a standard Purchase

Agreement (Offer for Purchase) that has been reviewed by several lawyers who have found it useful as the initial purchase document. Unlike a Letter of Intent, a Purchase Agreement is a binding contract that, when all the contingencies are satisfied, becomes the governing document.

Letters of Intent, on the other hand, are almost never binding and only touch on the more pertinent issues that are routinely addressed in a Purchase Agreement. For that reason, I discourage the use of Letters of Intent in favor of the Purchase Agreement that more aptly displays the true intent of the proposed transaction.

After due diligence and the purchaser's approval and acceptance of the vetted information, the earnest money deposit usually becomes non-refundable if the buyer decides to back out of the deal.

Following are some general guidelines regarding specific terms and conditions to be found in the Purchase Agreement **[pages 43 through 47]** to help you fill in the blanks.

PARAGRAPH #1 - DEPOSIT AND LIST OF ASSETS. Normally 2% to 5% of the total purchase price is a suitable earnest money deposit. The "ownership" of the business refers to the legal entity, not the individual owner, i.e., the corporation, partnership or limited liability company. The only time an individual's name appears on this line is when the business is a sole proprietorship.

As previously stated, the list of assets to be conveyed is vitally important because it specifically defines what the buyer is actually purchasing. All of the items listed in this paragraph are considered to be essential to the continuing operation of the business. In some cases, the seller may have a sentimental attachment to the business's name and ask that it not be included in the sale. The ONLY time this should be allowed is when the business is damaged by the name due to negative goodwill. Otherwise the name is an essential asset to the business's ongoing viability.

Some business web sites are owned by the host company that constructed the web site and are only leased to the business. That is why the conveyance language states that only the seller's ownership interest in the web site is being transferred.

If the business has equipment leases, they must be conveyed through lease assignments that become effective upon closing. Generally a phone call to the leasing company will generate the necessary paperwork for these assignments. It may be necessary to add other items to this paragraph, based on the final negotiations, such as the word, "franchise," if an existing franchise is being purchased.

PARAGRAPH #2 - TERMS. This contract assumes that the deal will be financed by the seller, which is the most prevalent small business acquisition scenario. However, in the event of a *cash* transaction, 2(a) would be changed to read, " Deposit on the date of this agreement included in the total Purchase Price," 2(b) would also be changed to read, " Balance of Purchase Price to be deposited in cash or certified funds, with Escrow Agent at closing," and 2(c) and 2(d) would be eliminated.

Returning to the seller-financed scenario, the purchase price should be expressed in writing as well as numerically. However, the down payment, number of years to pay off the note and interest rate can all be listed numerically. On line 2(a) the earnest money deposit should be repeated because it will be part of the down payment expressed on lines 2(b) and 2(c). Lines 2(a) and 2(b) should add up to the total down payment listed on line 2(c). Line 2(d) reflects the balance of the Purchase Price to be financed by the seller after the earnest money and down payment are deducted. This paragraph also defines the terms of payment, i.e., the monthly payment, number of payments due and interest rate. Today (circa 2014), the typical term is seven years and the going interest rate is six percent to seven percent. You can calculate the monthly payment by going on-line to one of several websites such as www.bankrate.com.

PARAGRAPH #3 - ESCROW/CLOSING. Seller-financed deals usually take no more than a month to close, but Franchises and SBA/Bank (cash) transactions may take more than two months (most franchises require the buyer to undergo extensive training prior to closing; SBA/bank-financed sales must wade through a quagmire of red tap before they are funded). The neutral Escrow Attorney will usually need about a week to prepare the closing documents and order both the chattel and tax lien searches to determine if there are any liens or encumbrances that might interfere with the conveyance of the assets and block the closing.

The escrow attorney can be any attorney willing to serve as a "neutral" party in the transaction, to prepare documents that are both fair and protective of both parties. The escrow attorneys I have used typically charged between $1,000.00 and $2,000.00 (circa 2014) to prepare the final closing documents. To ensure the closing attorney's neutrality, the attorney's fees are divided evenly between buyer and seller.

PARAGRAPH #4 - INVENTORY. This paragraph is only used when a buyer is purchasing a business that has either a raw material or finished goods inventory - usually retail, whole-sale or manufacturing businesses. The amount of inventory to be conveyed in a sale should be at a normal operating level, at the seller's cost, so the transaction is essentially turnkey, meaning all the components are in place to enable the buyer to begin operating the business immediately (and effectively) upon possession. If the Inventory shown in the Purchase Agreement differs from the actual inventory count taken just prior to closing, the purchase price and promissory note are adjusted accordingly. In the event of a *cash* sale only the purchase price is adjusted for any inventory variance.

It is customary for the Inventory to be counted by the buyer and seller. If an inventory counting service is used, the fee should be shared equally between the two parties and language to that effect should be inserted into Paragraph #4.

PARAGRAPH #5 - SELLER'S WARRANTIES. This paragraph outlines the protections afforded the buyer and Paragraph 5(c) allows the buyer to offset any damages incurred from a breach of these warranties against the seller's promissory note. For example, if a claim is made against the business as a result of some action (or inaction) taken by the seller prior to the closing, the buyer has the ability to contact the seller and ask for resolution, and if the obligation is not resolved within a reasonable period of time, to deduct the amount of the claim from future promissory note payments until the claim is satisfied. The concept of "offset" is the buyer's ultimate protection in a business sale transaction. The seller's ultimate protection is the buyer's personal guarantee on any promissory note or lease assignment.

In the event of a *cash* sale, the offset language in 5(c) can be changed to reflect the use of an *escrow account* rather than a promissory note. It is both fair and advisable for the buyer to ask that a portion of the seller's closing proceeds (usually ten percent to fifteen percent) be placed in an escrow account and that escrow instructions be incorporated into the closing documents allowing the buyer to offset any damages incurred after closing as expressed in the above paragraph. PARAGRAPH #6 - SCOPE OF AGREEMENT. This paragraph simply means that any changes to the Purchase Agreement must be in writing and agreed to by both parties, otherwise the Agreement stands as written.

PARAGRAPH #7 - CLIENT/VENDOR LISTS. This paragraph conveys to the buyer any and all customer and vendor lists - two of the most important intangible assets in a successful business.

PARAGRAPH #8 - LEASE. It's important that the lease term be at least as long as the financing commitment. This can be accomplished with a fixed-term lease, e.g., seven years, or a lease with options, e.g., an initial term of three years with two, two-year renewal options.

In the event of SBA/bank-financing, a ten-year lease may be required. This again can also be realized in segments, e.g., a base term of four years with two, three-year renewal options (or any other combination of fixed-term and renewals adding up to ten years that is acceptable to both landlord and tenant).

If the seller was initially required to provide a lease deposit, it will be the buyer's responsibility to replace that deposit at the closing. In most cases, a new lease or lease assignment [**see page 58**] is in place at the time of closing, BUT, the wording expressly states that the lease is null and void if the closing does not occur

PARAGRAPH #9 - DISPUTE RESOLUTION. The purpose of this paragraph is to help buyers and sellers resolve any disputes without having to resort to litigation. However, in the event the matter must be settled in court, this paragraph mandates that the loser will pay the winner's attorney's fees and court costs. This provision is designed to discourage frivolous or unnecessary lawsuits.

PARAGRAPH #10 - EXAMINATION OF BOOKS, RECORDS AND ASSETS. This paragraph defines the *due diligence* period during which a buyer may inspect or review anything he or she feels is pertinent to a comfortable and successful consummation of the purchase. The usual time frame for due diligence is two to three weeks but additional time may be needed with complex businesses.

This is one of the most critical periods in the business buying process and the buyer is encouraged to ask for an accountant's assistance. It is the seller's obligation to provide all of the information requested by the buyer in a timely manner in order to keep the deal on track.

Once the buyer is satisfied that the business's financial records and assets are as represented by the seller, the buyer will likely be asked to sign a release of this contingency, thereby making the earnest money non-refundable. At that time, the Purchase Agreement is usually turned over to the closing attorney for preparation of final closing documents. The language for the removal of the *due diligence* contingency is as follows:

CONTINGENCY REMOVAL FORM

TO WHOM IT MAY CONCERN: **I/We, the undersigned Buyer(s)** of that certain business known as:

Business Name: _____

Located at: _____, City, State, Zip

hereby remove the following contingency on that certain Offer to Purchase dated _____, 20__ which reads:

> Paragraph 10. EXAMINATION OF BOOKS RECORDS AND ASSETS. "Purchaser shall have _____ (_) days after Seller's acceptance of this Offer to Purchase, and after gaining access to the following items, to complete an examination of the furniture, fixtures, equipment, books, records, workers' compensation history, contracts and such other information deemed pertinent to the Seller's business by Purchaser, and Purchaser will rely solely on that personal inspection in making this Offer to Purchase. In the event this Contingency is not removed in writing by the end of the examination period, this Offer to Purchase shall be terminated and the Purchaser's Deposit shall be refunded. "

It is understood by the parties hereto, that upon the execution of this release of contingency, Purchaser's earnest money shall be deemed non-refundable.

All other terms and conditions of the Offer to Purchase will remain unchanged. Receipt of a copy of this Contingency Removal Form is hereby acknowledged.

_____   _____
Purchaser   Purchaser

_____   _____
Date   Date

PARAGRAPH #11 - TRAINING AND CONSULTING. A typical training period for a non-technical business is one to two months, followed by a three to six-month consulting period. If the business is especially complicated or its success is due to close personal relationships between the seller and the customer base, a longer transition period will likely be required. In some extreme cases, such as the sale of a professional practice (accountant, medical, insurance, etc.), it is not unusual for the buyer to insist on as much as a year of on-site consulting. It is normal for the buyer to expect the seller to spend at least four to six hours, per normal work day, in the business during the initial training period. Such short-term training and consulting are typically free. If the sale requires some long-term involvement on the part of the seller, a compensation package can usually be negotiated.

In the sale of an existing franchise, the franchisor will likely require the buyer to attend the franchisor's training school prior to closing, which can last as little as a week or as long as two months, depending on the complexity of the franchise. This additional time frame must be addressed when choosing a closing date (see Paragraph #3).

PARAGRAPH #12 - ASSIGNMENT OF CONTRACTS. The buyer has the right to ask the seller for the assignment of all contracts relating to the business that the buyer feels will help ensure the business's future success. This may include equipment leases, Yellow Page contract, service contracts, vendor agreements, website hosting contracts, etc. The seller should be asked for a complete list of any such contracts, leases or agreements during due diligence.

PARAGRAPH #13 - COVENANT NOT TO COMPETE. Every business sale should include a covenant not to compete that prevents the seller from starting or purchasing a similar business within the current business's market area. In the event the seller has multiple competing businesses, the non-compete agreement must be carefully structured to protect the buyer from further infringement in the subject business's market area.

A non-compete agreement must contain three components to be enforceable: time, area and compensation. The typical time frame for a non-compete agreement is five years and it should cover the market area currently being served by the business. This can be expressed in terms of the general area surrounding the business, e.g. within a two-mile radius of the business; or a geographic delineation, e.g., the county, city or state in which the business operates.

If the non-compete agreement is overstated (any extreme or broad interpretation of distance, e.g., the entire state for a neighborhood restaurant), or time, e.g., ten or more years, it may render the non-compete agreement unenforceable. This paragraph covers time and distance while the compensation component is defined in paragraph #15 [Allocations]. It is important to note that regardless of the amount of money that is allocated to the non-compete agreement in paragraph #15, it does not the limit the damages that a court may award the buyer in the event of a breach of the non-compete.

PARAGRAPH #14 - NAME CHANGE. In cases where the name of the business is similar to that of the legal entity, e.g., Acme Window, Inc. doing business as Acme Window, the seller needs to change the name of the legal entity immediately after closing so there is no confusion on the part of the public, the government or financial institutions as to the new ownership.

PARAGRAPH #15 - ALLOCATIONS. Buyers and seller may wish to talk to their accountants about this paragraph, as both parties must agree on the Allocations for tax purposes. Most buyers use the Furniture, Fixtures, Equipment and Inventory figures from the marketing brochure or package for those two figures. The Non-compete portion shouldn't be much more than twenty percent of the purchase price in order to satisfy the IRS, and the Goodwill usually covers the balance required so the Allocations add up to the total purchase price.

Sellers like to allocate as much of the purchase price as possible to *goodwill* because it is treated as capital gains, resulting in a lesser tax than is assessed ordinary income. Buyers, on the other hand, prefer to allocate as much of the purchase price as possible to furniture, fixtures and equipment, because these hard assets can be depreciated over time and provide a tax write-off.

PARAGRAPH #16 - CASH/ACCOUNTS RECEIVABLE /ACCOUNTS PAYABLE. In most business sales, the seller retains the existing cash and accounts receivable and retires any accounts payable and other debts that exist at time of closing. However, in some cases, where the buyer is willing to reimburse the seller for cash and accounts receivable and assume the seller's accounts payable and other debt in order to maintain the existing cash flow, this paragraph must be rewritten to reflect those changes. In these situations, the buyer and seller should agree on a baseline figure for both the accounts receivable and accounts payable and then adjust the seller's promissory note at a later date (usually after ninety days) for any difference between the agreed-upon baseline amount and what was actually collected as accounts receivable or paid as accounts payable.

For example, if at the time of closing the Cash and Accounts Receivable total $50,000 and the Accounts Payable and other debt total $40,000, the Buyer would have to pay the seller the $10,000 difference at closing. After ninety days, if the buyer was able to collect all but $5,000 of the outstanding Accounts Receivable, the $5,000 difference would be deducted from the seller's promissory note. The seller would then be allowed to pursue the delinquent accounts through legal channels.

PARAGRAPH #17 - FINANCING. If institutional financing is required in lieu of a seller-held note, the buyer should allow about three to five weeks for a bank to make its loan commitment. As previously stated, SBA/bank financing can take as long as two months to secure, so the closing date should reflect this added time. If the sale is to be seller-financed, this paragraph should be expunged.

PARAGRAPH #18 - ACCEPTANCE OF OFFER. A typical response period is three to five days from the time the broker submits the buyer's offer to the seller. Additional time may be requested if the seller wishes to have the offer reviewed by an attorney or some other entity.

CHAPTER ELEVEN:

THE ASSET PURCHASE AGREEMENT

1. DEPOSIT. Received from_____, or Assigns (herein, "PURCHASER"), on _____, 20__, the sum of _____ _____ Thousand and no/100 Dollars ($_____.00) in the form of a check as an earnest money deposit (herein, "Deposit") on the purchase price of all furniture, fixtures, equipment, leases, goodwill, inventory, trademarks, telephone numbers, the Yellow Pages advertising contract through its current term, trade names, web site (to the extent of Seller's ownership interest), client lists and other tangible and intangible assets of that Business

known as: _____ (herein, "Business"),

owned by: _____ (herein, "Seller"), and

located at: _____

PURCHASER AND SELLER do hereby, jointly and severally, direct and authorize _____, (herein, "Escrow Agent") to deposit amounts of earnest money, and hold same in Escrow Agent's trust account.

2. TERMS. The total Purchase Price of _____Thousand and No/100 dollars ($_____.00) shall be paid as follows:

a. $_____.00 Deposit on the date of this agreement included in down payment.

b. $_____.00 Balance of down payment to be deposited in cash or certified funds, with Escrow Agent at closing.

c. $_____.00 Total Down Payment.

d. $_____.00 Balance of Purchase Price to be paid to the Seller pursuant to a Secured Promissory Note ("Seller's Note") in said amount, payable at $_____.00, or more per month for __ months, with interest thereon at ___% per annum, together with a security agreement and a financing statement as provided by the Uniform Commercial Code of the State of _____ which shall be filed with the appropriate State Agency. **Said Promissory Note shall include the Purchaser's personal guarantee.**

$_____.00 TOTAL PURCHASE PRICE

3. ESCROW/CLOSING. For the purpose of completing this transaction, escrow shall be opened at the office of _____Escrow Agent and closing shall take place on or before 3:00 P.M. on _____, 20__. Escrow Agent is hereby authorized to prepare the necessary closing documents for the consummation of this transaction. All closing costs, including Escrow Agent's fees, shall be paid equally by Seller and Purchaser.

4. INVENTORY. The Purchase Price includes an allocation of $_____.00 for Inventory valued at Seller's cost. If actual Inventory is determined to be more or less than that amount, the Purchase Price and Seller's Note will be adjusted accordingly. Inventory is to be counted and priced by Seller and Purchaser.

5. SELLER'S WARRANTIES. Seller hereby warrants that:

    a. At the time of physical possession by Purchaser, all of the Business equipment will be in good working order and will pass all inspections necessary to conduct such business. Possession of the equipment shall take place at closing.

    b. It has good, clear, recorded, and marketable title to all of the Business assets being conveyed in this transaction as mentioned above.

    c. All representations made to Purchaser by Seller regarding this transaction are true and accurate to the best of Seller's knowledge, and Seller grants Purchaser the right to set off any damages suffered by

Purchaser, as a result of any breach of any of the Seller's warranties or representations, against Seller's Note.

    d. To the best of Seller's knowledge, the above Business, its assets, and its leasehold are in full compliance with all federal, state, and municipal laws, rules, ordinances, regulations, and requirements, and there has been no spill or discharge of any hazardous substance or waste on those premises.

6. SCOPE OF AGREEMENT. This Agreement, and any other exhibits and addenda attached hereto and any documents subsequently signed by the parties, constitute the entire Agreement; there are no oral agreements, understandings or representations being relied upon by the parties; and all prior negotiations, agreements and understandings, written or verbal, are superseded by this Agreement. Any modifications must be in writing and signed by all the parties to this Agreement. Should there be any conflict between the provisions of this Agreement and any escrow instructions executed pursuant hereto, the provisions of the final Closing Documents shall control.

7. CLIENT/VENDOR LISTS. Seller agrees to deliver all lists of Clients and Vendors to Purchaser at time of closing.

8. LEASE. Seller leases the premises where the Business is conducted and the Purchaser is not obligated to close unless the Seller delivers, at closing, a suitable new Lease, assignment of the existing lease or a sublease, with respect to the Business premises having a term of not less than _____ (__) months at a base rent of $_____.00 per month. Purchaser will have five (5) days after receipt of a copy of the new Lease, Assignment of existing Lease or Sublease to reject it, or it will be deemed approved. If Purchaser rejects, or Seller is unable to deliver a suitable new Lease, Assignment of the existing Lease or Sublease, this Offer to Purchase will be terminated and Purchaser's Deposit will be refunded.

9. DISPUTE RESOLUTION. If a dispute arises out of or relates to this Agreement or its breach, the Seller and Purchaser (and Broker, if any) shall endeavor to settle the dispute through direct discussions. If the dispute cannot be settled through direct discussions, Seller and

Purchaser (and Broker, if any) shall endeavor to settle the dispute through arbitration before recourse to litigation. The location of the arbitration shall be in _____ or such other location as agreed to by Seller and Purchaser. Seller and Purchaser (and Broker, if any) further agree, that in the event any litigation is instituted to enforce or interpret any of the provisions of this Agreement or for any other reasons, the prevailing party shall be entitled to recover from the other its reasonable attorney's fees and court costs, including appeals, as determined by the Court in such action or suit.

10. **EXAMINATION OF BOOKS, RECORDS AND ASSETS.** Purchaser shall have _____ (__) days after Seller's acceptance of this Offer to Purchase, and after gaining access to the following items, to complete an examination of the furniture, fixtures, equipment, books, records, workers' compensation history, contracts, and such other information deemed pertinent to Seller's business by Purchaser, and Purchaser will rely solely on that personal inspection in making this Offer to Purchase. In the event this contingency is not removed in writing by the end of the examination period, this Offer to Purchase shall be terminated and Purchaser's Deposit shall be refunded. [See language to remove this contingency on page 40].

11. **TRAINING AND CONSULTING.** Seller agrees to train Purchaser in the operation of the Business, at no additional charge to purchaser, for a period of _____ (__) weeks from closing. Training shall take place at the Business location and shall consist of a minimum of _____ (__) hours per day. No training will be required of Seller on weekends. Following the initial training period, Seller will act as consultant to Purchaser for a period of _____ (__) additional months - consulting to be performed by Seller primarily by telephone.

12. **ASSIGNMENT OF CONTRACT(S).** Seller hereby agrees to assign all rights to the Purchaser, in any contracts benefiting Purchaser, including but not limited to those dealing with: Yellow Pages advertising, web site maintenance, equipment maintenance and service, vendor discounts, etc., that exist at time of closing.

13. COVENANT NOT TO COMPETE. Seller hereby agrees not to compete with Purchaser, either directly or indirectly in the operation of the above Business, for a period of _____ (__) years from date of closing, and in an area defined as _____.

14. NAME CHANGE. In the event Seller's corporate name is the same or very similar to the name of the business being conveyed, Seller hereby agrees to either change the name of its corporation, or dissolve the corporation, no later than thirty (30) days following closing.

15. ALLOCATIONS. Seller and Purchaser agree that the Purchase Price shall be allocated as follows:
    a) Furniture, Fixtures & Equipment $_____.00
    b) Inventory   _____.00
    c) Non-compete Agreement   _____.00
    d) Goodwill, Client Lists, etc.   _____.00

        Total: $

16. CASH/ACCOUNTS RECEIVABLE/ACCOUNTS PAYABLE. At closing, Seller shall retain all Cash on Hand and Accounts Receivable, and further agrees to pay all Accounts Payable and other debts or encumbrances against the above Business unless otherwise specified in this Agreement.

17. FINANCING. This sale is contingent upon Purchaser being able to secure suitable financing from a bona fide lending institution within _____ days from the date of this Offer to Purchase. If Purchaser is unable to obtain a financing commitment within this period of time, this Offer to Purchase will be terminated and Purchaser's Deposit will be refunded.

18. ACCEPTANCE OF OFFER. When signed by the Purchaser, this deposit receipt is an Offer to Purchase the above business on terms stated, and should Seller fail to accept this offer by signature hereon prior to 6:00 p.m., _____, 20__, this Offer to Purchase will be terminated and Purchaser's Deposit will be refunded. [In the event a Broker is involved, the following language should be added: "Upon

Seller's acceptance of this Offer to Purchase, Seller hereby directs Broker not to advise or present Seller with any subsequent offer(s) received by Broker until after forfeiture by the Purchaser or other nullification of this Offer to Purchase"].

****

PURCHASER and SELLER individually acknowledge the receipt of a copy of this Agreement. This is a legally binding document. Please read it carefully. If you do not understand it, consult an attorney.

****

PURCHASER hereby agrees to buy the Business on the terms set forth above.

Dated: _____, 20___ At: _____AM _____PM

Purchaser:_____

Address: _____

Signature(s): _____

SELLER hereby agrees to sell the Business on the terms set forth above.

Dated: _____, 20___ At: _____AM _____PM

Seller: _____

Address: _____

Signature: _____

Note: If no broker is being utilized in the proposed transaction, all references to a "broker" should be removed from the Purchase Agreement.

DISCLAIMER: This Offer for Purchase and Sale of Assets, Earnest Money Receipt and Agreement (Purchase Agreement) has been in use for more than thirty years in the author's home state of New Mexico and has undergone several modifications and updates by New Mexico attorneys and accountants. The author does not guarantee either its legality or functionality in any other venue. However, in the author's best judgment, all of the warranties, representations, conditions and contingencies that are expressed in this Purchase Agreement should be included, in some manner, in every purchase agreement regardless of the venue or jurisdiction.

As is the case with all legal documents, this Purchase Agreement should be reviewed by an attorney knowledgeable in contract and business law.

CHAPTER TWELVE:

THE SELLER'S ROLE IN DUE DILIGENCE

Assuming the buyer has made an acceptable Offer to Purchase, the task of Due Diligence will begin. In this phase of the negotiations, the buyer will provide a list of all of the books, records and other information that the buyer wants to review. It is incumbent upon the seller to provide everything the buyer requests, within reason of course, to maintain the buyer's interest and comfort in consummating the acquisition.

The obvious items, such as books and records, can be easily obtained from the company bookkeeper or accountant. Other tangible items, such as equipment and inventory, can be inspected at the buyer's and seller's leisure at the business premises. However, certain non-tangible issues, such as the retention of key employees and clients, require a different approach.

No seller wants to subject clients or employees to buyer scrutiny, but in some cases, it's the only way to assure a buyer that the business will continue to run as advertised. If the business has only a limited clientele, any prudent buyer will want some assurance that the primary customer base will continue to do business with the company post sale. This is generally not an issue with a large client base.

The same is true if there are key employees who are capable of running the business once the seller retires (especially if the buyer is unfamiliar with the basic underpinnings of the business).

In these two examples, a buyer will ask for a meeting with either the more substantial customers or key employees. In order to preserve as much of the seller's confidentiality as possible, these meetings should not take place until _all_ of the other sale contingencies have been satisfied, and then only under the scrutiny of the seller. The reason behind this cautionary approach can best be explained through the following story:

I sold a large commercial floral maintenance business to its major competitor. Because the two companies had vied for each others' customers for more than ten years, a strong rivalry brewed not only between the owners, but also the employees. For this reason, the buyer asked for a meeting with the key employees as his last contract contingency. The seller reluctantly agreed and I arranged the meeting with seven key department managers.

I offered the buyer some "coaching" as to how he should address the employees, e.g., *"I value you and look forward to working with you, etc."* Unfortunately, the buyer looked around the room and exclaimed, "Next week you will all be working for me and then you will discover what real work is!" All seven managers flew off their chairs and literally ran out the door - followed closely behind by the enraged seller. The erstwhile buyer simply looked at me and stated, "See, I told you they wouldn't work for me!" Fortunately, the seller was able to corral his employees, promising them he would never sell to that #!&* individual. Luckily, I was able to sell the business to a quality individual a week later, who never requested a meeting and was embraced by the employees after the closing (probably because they were still having nightmares over their previous encounter).

If the sale of the business is contingent on the buyer contacting some key customers, it should not occur until just prior to closing and, as previously stated, after all the other contingencies have been satisfied. It is an unrealistic expectation for the buyer to want to meet or converse with all the customers, so such meetings should be limited to only the top two or three customers. The introductions should be structured in such a way that the customers understand that the seller is *considering* selling a significant interest in the business and the buyer wants to know if the customers are satisfied with the services or products rendered and will likely continue to do business with the company if there are no substantive changes. The fact that the interest being sold is 100% does not constitute misinformation because 100% is very significant.

In another example of employee retention, an absentee owner (call him Bob) hired and trained a young man (call him Stan) to operate his labor-intensive business once he felt he was too old to handle the day-to-day physical requirements. When Bob decided to put his business up for sale, he was fully aware of the major role his hired hand would play in the wooing of a potential buyer. In fact, he was justifiably concerned over the possibility that his highly-trained employee would go into business for himself by stealing the business's customers. Since the employee was the de-facto *face* of the business, that task could have been easily accomplished.

When Bob asked for my advice, I told him to try to purchase some time from Stan by offering him some contingent compensation...in other words, a bribe. After meeting with Stan and telling him of his decision to sell - and offering Stan the first chance at an offer, Stan expressed his intention to compete. Bob then asked what it would take for Stan to remain with the business for six months until a buyer was trained and in control. The price of "loyalty" was a new Ford F-150 pickup with all the bells and whistles. Bob had no choice but to agree to the deal if he wanted to retire.

In short order, a buyer was found who was willing to pay the purchase price of close to $100,000 as long as Stan trained him and stayed with the business for at least six months. Fortunately, during the four-month training period, both Bob and the buyer worked diligently to establish the buyer as a professional capable of operating the business. They did this through frequent customer contacts and faster than promised service. Because Bob made the original customer contacts several years earlier, he was a respected and recognizable figure, and when he asked the customers to support the new owner, they responded in a positive manner. Subsequently, Stan, although more knowledgeable about the business than the buyer, was unable to steer away a single customer after the training period. At last report, Stan is still working for the expanded business and proudly driving his Ford F-150 pickup.

CHAPTER THIRTEEN:

THE CATCH 22 OF SELLING "CASH" BUSINESSES

"I want a business that generates lots of cash!"

This is a familiar refrain heard by business brokers throughout the country - a request from buyers looking for businesses where the customers pay in cash as opposed to checks or credit cards - cash that can be "creatively sheltered" from the grasp of the IRS. Cash businesses are easily identifiable: laundromats, bars, restaurants, convenience stores, gas stations, small retail establishments and any other businesses that rely on a large number of cash sales. It is no secret that some of the cash generated by these businesses never shows up in the stores' cash register receipts or profit and loss statements. But apart from being an act of tax defiance, there are other, long-term ramifications to consider before "stealing" from one's own business?

One potential rude awakening occurs when these business owners decide to sell their "discretely profitable" businesses. In establishing the value of a business, cash flow is king, not hidden cash! When the cash flow, i.e. true profit, is hidden, so is the value of the enterprise.

I once met an owner of a cash-generating business doing about a half million in actual sales, but showing only $455,000 on his tax return. Like most business owners, he wanted to sell his enterprise for the highest possible price so he could retire in style. Although he had the higher sales figure documented in an obscure notebook, it didn't make any difference in my evaluation, which relies on provable numbers - numbers that can be substantiated by the tax return (signed under penalty of perjury). Unfortunately, due to his limited provable cash flow, my evaluation came out less than what we knew was the real value of his business.

Faced with this dilemma, some owners have asked me to leave them alone with the prospective buyer so they can show them the *real* numbers." The only reasonable response to this illogical and potentially dangerous suggestion is, "Life is too short to spend it fighting the IRS." It would be absurd for any owner to turn over a second set of books to a perfect stranger, yet it is done every day, throughout the country, by business owners more focused on price than self preservation.

In another, slightly more covert approach, owners encourage prospective buyers to "monitor" the traffic and sales of the subject business over a fixed period of time. This method is intended to show would-be buyers that the number of customers times the average sales ticket equals the true sales volume of the business for that period. Unfortunately, this approach does not take into account such variables as seasonal fluctuations, sales promotions, economic cycles or the seller's ability to muster his friends and relatives into an army of short-term customers. And while we're on the subject of cash-generating businesses, another potential problem is the propensity for that cash to slip into employees' pockets before it can be ensconced in the owner's. Most owners of cash businesses agree that they have to maintain a strong presence in the business every hour it is open in order to guard the cash - a sad but true reflection of our society.

It is fair to conclude that owners of cash businesses must make a choice: whether to enjoy preferred tax treatment during their terms of ownership and forego the true value of their enterprise at the time of sale; or pay the piper (IRS) its due each year and receive a fair market price.

Conservative owners tend to pay the piper while their more liberal counterparts perceive their cake as forever whole even though they constantly nibble at it. Moderates, on the other hand, eat away for five years, stop eating for a couple of years, and then sell their *reconstituted* cake at close to full value.

A business broker can only sell what a seller can prove.

CHAPTER FOURTEEN:

EARN-OUTS

Buyers will sometimes ask for an "earn-out" as part of the terms of sale because it allows them to acquire a business at a low price while offering the seller some upside potential if the business meets certain levels of success.

In an earn-out, a *target* price is established that is generally more than the original asking price. The eventual purchase price is usually far below the *target* price and the buyer makes a reasonable down payment to offset some of the seller's fears. For the seller to receive the difference between the purchase price and the *target* price, the buyer must be able to meet certain challenges such as renewing key contracts or improving sales and cash flow that existed at time of closing. As contracts renew and cash flow improves (with the seller's assistance), the seller usually receives a fixed percentage of the difference between the initial price paid and the *target* price. Another possible *upside* in an earn-out might involve the seller's ability to obtain some new contracts that had been in negotiations prior to the sale and for which a commission or "finder's fee" might be paid to the seller once the contract is secured.

Most business brokers represent sellers in a transaction - not buyers. When confronted with an "earn-out" offer, brokers invariably advise their sellers not to entertain it. The seller generally receives similar advice from his or her accountant and attorney, because in an earn-out, the buyer has all the control, and if the buyer is unscrupulous, the books and records can be "adjusted" to reflect the buyer's best interests. This chapter is not designed to dissuade sellers from this course of action but to let them understand the odds that are stacked against them. In my thirty-year career, I have only done a couple of earn-outs - the last one in 2010.

Earn-outs may be an acceptable course of action when the business being acquired is in dire straits and no other buyers are coming forward to make an offer. In such cases, the seller may be willing to roll the dice to try to recover some return on the time, money and effort that has been put into the business and possible keep the business afloat and long-time employees on the payroll.

In order to offset the inherent earn-out risk, a seller needs to balance the scales with a potentially greater reward. Therefore, the deal must be attractive enough that the seller believes there is a reasonable chance of getting more than the bare bones purchase price.

An example of a typical earn-out involves a real company that was once successful, but as the ownership aged, became a victim of lethargy. The business's negative cash flow meant that its de facto value was whatever its assets would bring on the open market... around $250,000. Because of the once profitable contracts still in place and the tried and true employees, a company that was in the same business in another part of the country, found the acquisition attractive. However, knowing it would take thousands of dollars to turn the business around, an earn-out seemed to be the only feasible buy-out option available.

After the parties agreed to no down payment, the off-setting target price was set at $500,000. Once the business realized its break-even point, the profits were to be split seventy-thirty, with the lower percentage going to the seller. This arrangement was to continue for five years or until the $500,000 target price was reached, whichever came first. Fortunately, at the end of five years the sellers had been paid and the business and its employees were part of a solid and growing company.

This example obviously only shows the upside of an earn-out and doesn't address the ones that don't work out...which I believe are more prevalent.

CHAPTER FIFTEEN:

RETAIL BUSINESSES - LIQUIDATION OR SALE

What should you do when it comes time to for you to retire from a retail business? PricewaterhouseCoopers, an international professional services company conducted a study of the retail industry to explore how retail stores are sold. It surveyed respondents operating approximately 12,000 stores and looked at a variety of means employed to sell the inventory and assets of retail stores, including the following four primary methods:

> 1. Going Concern Sale – A store is sold to a purchaser who intends to continue operating it as a business and is willing to pay for some "goodwill" over and above the value of the assets.

> 2. Bulk Sale – Inventory, equipment and other assets are sold in lots to another retail business owner for resale.

> 3. Auction Sale – Inventory and other assets (furniture, fixtures and equipment) are organized in lots and sold at auction.

> 4. Store Closing Sale – Inventory and assets are liquidated in a going-out-of-business sale.

In my experience, methods #1 and #4 appear to be the most popular. Retail businesses with large inventories sometimes have a higher asset value than the appraised value based on the store's cash flow. This is especially true if the owner has been pumping profits back into the business to build up the inventory.

I was once asked to evaluate a card and gift store that had inventory of $200,000 but a cash flow of only $25,000. Over their five-year ownership period, the proprietors had taken little salary, choosing instead to plow most of their profits back into inventory.

Unfortunately, even if the sellers could realize the value of their inventory in a *Going Concern Sale*, the $25,000 *provable* cash flow was insufficient to retire that much debt and still pay the buyer a salary or any return on investment.

In situations like this, it is often a strategic alternative to sell off the assets through an orderly liquidation (*Store Closing Sale*). In many such cases, a retailer will purchase additional inventory to showcase during the liquidation process. The words, "Liquidation Sale - Everything Must Go," are great attention-getters and will drive traffic to a store when all other "motivators" fail.

In a *going concern sale*, inventory is conveyed "at cost" (what the seller paid for the inventory). However, in a Store Closing Sale, an owner often offers discounts of 20% to 30% at the beginning of the sale. If a piece of inventory cost the seller $50.00 and was priced to sell at $100.00 (a typical keystone markup), a 30% discount would equate to a $70.00 selling price…$20 more than the owner would have realized on that item if it were included in the price of the business as a going concern. Even at a 50% discount, the owner will recover all the money that has been diverted to inventory rather than to his or her pockets.

Two other advantages of a Store Closing Sale include: a predictable store closing date and all sales are in cash and/or credit cards with no accounts receivable. There are liquidation companies whose sole purpose is to help retailers plan and execute Store Closing Sales (for a fee, of course) to maximize the owner's return. One such company provides an on-site consultant to analyze the best timing for a Store Closing Sale, anticipate the return, contact media reps, train employees, price the merchandise and survey the competition.

On the other hand, if a business generates sufficient cash flow to substantiate a *goodwill* figure over and above the wholesale value of the inventory and other assets, an owner should consider a *going concern sale*. Two obvious advantages of this type of transaction are:

> 1. The business continues in operation, which often has an emotional value that is priceless to the entrepreneur who

started it.

2. The employees retain their jobs, which is often a major concern to an owner with loyal, long-term employees.

Another factor impacting the decision may be the presence of an existing lease. If the business owner is the personal guarantor on a lease with five years left, he or she will have to either make arrangements with the landlord to retire that obligation early, or sell the business as a going concern with the buyer taking over the remaining lease obligation.

In either case, this is a major decision in the life of every retailer and deserves both serious study and professional assistance.

CHAPTER SIXTEEN:

THE SELLER'S LEASE CONCERNS

About twenty years ago, I received a call from a restaurateur (let's call him Jim) who wanted to sell his business. He had been in business in the same location for more than a decade and he wanted to reap the fruits of his labor and retire. Unfortunately, Jim failed to renew his lease two years earlier and had been on month-to-month status ever since.

When I secured an acceptable offer, I accompanied Jim and the purchaser to his landlord to negotiate a new lease. Unfortunately, the landlord had other thoughts regarding the property's future. His son had recently returned to New Mexico from a stint in the Army and was seeking gainful employment.

The landlord, who knew that Jim had built a prosperous business in his building, decided that he would take advantage of Jim's enterprise and turn the site over to his son. Used restaurant equipment is fairly cheap, so he knew if Jim removed his furniture, fixtures and equipment after being evicted, his son could have the restaurant reopened in less than a month. When Jim protested, his arguments went unheeded. His landlord had made up his mind and all Jim had to show for his years in business was some used furniture and equipment, a refrigerator half full of food and some dog-eared menus. The landlord's son took over the site, prred similar food and prospered by serving Jim's old clientele (so much for customer loyalty).

Jim's lackadaisical attitude regarding his lease cost him a comfortable retirement and forced him to relocate to another, less desirable site that never produced the same profits as his old location.

This outcome could have been averted with this **lease preventative maintenance program**:

1. **Plan ahead**. Make a note to remind yourself to start the renewal process at least two full years prior to the expiration date of your lease. Read your lease carefully, understand your renewal options (if any) and determine whether or not you want to remain in that location for another lease period. This may be a good time to research more desirable sites without fear of losing your existing location.

2. **Get help**. Seek the assistance of a commercial leasing agent specializing in the type of lease you require. A leasing professional will ask you to sign a Tenant Representation Agreement in order to protect his or her interest in any potential transaction commission. This is generally an exclusive agreement, so choose your agent carefully. Exclusivity is not a negative because it also mandates accountability to you on the part of your agent.

3. **Know your needs**. Give your agent all of your leasing criteria so a thorough search can be made of any comparable sites that might prove more advantageous or at least provide some leverage for negotiations with your current landlord.

4. **Stay Neutral**. Let your agent negotiate a new lease or extension of your existing lease. Having a third party negotiate on your behalf enables you to remain "politically neutral" while your agent endures the adversarial trauma. A professional, armed with current market data, who is arguing key points from a position of knowledge rather than emotion, also creates a more businesslike atmosphere. Best of all, many commission agreements provide for the tenant representative's fee is to be paid by the landlord as part of the normal transactional costs.

5. **The business sale scenario**. When a business owner decides to sell, there are some totally different concerns to be addressed. Most sellers don't want to remain on the lease once their business has sold, so they need to plan ahead. The ideal scenario for the seller involves the sale of the business near the end of a lease term but with protective renewal options in place. In this scenario, the seller introduces the business buyer to the landlord and the landlord and buyer negotiate a brand new lease and the seller has no further duties or responsibilities to the landlord.

When two or more years remain on the seller's lease, the landlord will understandably be reluctant to replace the seller, if the seller has consistently met all of the lease terms and conditions. The buyer, on the other hand, is an unknown entity. In these situations, the landlord will likely insist on an *Assignment of Lease*. Under this scenario, the buyer can be protected by going to the landlord and asking for a renewal option to be included in the Assignment of Lease so that additional future years may be added to the lease at the buyer's option.

Sellers should not expect their landlords to let them off their leases in the event of a sale of their business...there is simply no good reason for a landlord to do so. There is one positive aspect of a lease assignment for the seller: the seller is notified if the buyer is in default on the lease. Since most sales involve the seller carrying some portion of the financing, it is in the seller's best interests to know the status of the lease until the promissory note is paid. Most closing documents state that a default on the lease also constitutes a default on the seller's note. This way the seller can step in to either assist the buyer or make plans to take back the business before it is unsalvageable or there is no lease in place.

Business owners sometimes overlook their leases in lieu of the more immediate and demanding day-to-day operations. However, a $350,000 investment in inventory, equipment and leasehold improvements can be dwarfed by a bad lease - or even worse -the cost of having no lease at all.

Following is a typical lease assignment document:

ASSIGNMENT OF LEASE

[Some Lease Assignments require a notary public to witness the signatures of both the buyer and seller - the landlord's signature does not generally have to be notarized]

      For valuable consideration, we do hereby assign, set over and transfer unto _____(Buyer)_____ (herein, the "Assignee"), all of our rights, title and interest in and to that certain Lease dated _____, 20__, between _____ (herein, the "Landlord"), and _____ (herein, the "Tenant"), covering the premises located at _____(Address)_____(City, State, Zip)_____, known as _____(Business Name)_____, and subject to the same terms and conditions of the Lease therein set out, which the Assignee hereby assumes and agrees to perform all the covenants, terms, and conditions of the Lease on the part of the Tenant therein named to be performed.

      Dated this ___th day of _____, 20___.

_____
STATE OF _____)   Tenant
) ss.
COUNTY OF _____)

_____
                                                  Tenant

The foregoing instrument was acknowledged before me this ___the day of _____, 20__, by _____.

My Commission Expires: _____. _____
                                                             Notary Public

CONSENT OF ASSIGNEE

I/We, _____(Buyer)_____ do hereby accept the foregoing Assignment and hereby assume and agree to perform all of the terms, covenants and conditions of the Lease therein described on the part of the Tenant therein named to be performed. It is understood and agreed, that in the event the purchase of the business known as _____ is not consummated, this acceptance of the foregoing Assignment is null and void.

Dated this ____th day of _____, 20__.

STATE OF _____)
) ss.
COUNTY OF _____)

_____
Buyer/Assignee

_____
Buyer/Assignee

The foregoing instrument was acknowledged before me this ___ the day of _____, 20__, by _____.

My Commission Expires: _____. _____
                                                                    Notary Public

CONSENT OF LANDLORD

The above Assignment is consented to by the undersigned Landlord, upon the condition, however, that the said Assignment shall not release, relieve, or in any manner modify the obligations of _____(Seller)_____, Tenant, under the terms and conditions of said Lease.

Dated this ___th day of _____, 20__.

By:_____   _____
    Landlord   Attest

CHAPTER SEVENTEEN:

AVOID BIDDING WARS

There are some business brokers who advocate not setting a price on the business but letting the market dictate the price. This strategy often leads to a bidding war between would-be buyers who initially sense a bargain basement price that suddenly erupts into the stratosphere when emotions heat up. That may be a reasonable strategy for large businesses with multi-million dollar price tags and teams of advisors, but for the ordinary small business, it seldom works.

The reason is, both buyers and sellers of small businesses are usually *first-timers* with no hidden agendas. They simply want to consummate a win-win transaction that will provide both parties with a profitable and enjoyable future.

I recall a deal I was involved in back in the nineties, where in spite of the fact the seller and I had set the price and terms in our Listing Agreement, two potential buyers became involved in a bidding war - a result of having two other business brokers involved. Both brokers obviously wanted to get the deal done for their respective clients and to earn the resulting commission, so both encouraged their clients to *chase* the deal.

As a result, I received two offers within a day of each other, and since the seller had not yet accepted the first offer, I was duty-bound to present the newer/higher offer. It is very important to state at this time that **neither of the two brokers knew the details of the other broker's offer**.

The seller, with two offers in hand, was justifiably elated, and decided to encourage a bidding war. Against my advice, he called up the business broker with the lower offer and explained the details of the competitive bid. The first buyer came back to the table with a slightly higher bid than the second buyer...and the war commenced. A

$400,000 deal morphed into $450,000 before the war ended and the first buyer claimed victory. But the victory came at a cost of $50,000 more than the original listing price - which grated against the successful bidder's sense of fairness, until, for very little cause during the due diligence process, he decided to back out of the deal.

The panicky seller asked that I go back to the other broker and see if his client would like to buy the business at the **reduced** price of $425,000. If *hell hath no fury like a woman scorned*, I'd hate to see an analogy to a business buyer scorned. I was told, in no uncertain terms, what I could do with the seller's *reduced* offering. The end result was that both buyers left the table and the seller ultimately sold his business for $350,000.

It is an accepted axiom amongst business brokers that the first offer that a seller receives is often the best. So how should this scenario have played out to the seller's advantage?

The seller should have responded to the initial buyer's offer with a counter offer at or near the original list price. If the initial buyer refused to accept the counter offer, the seller could have approached the second buyer with either an acceptance or a counter offer, also at or near the list price. In this scenario, neither buyer feels "played."

If the initial buyer accepts the terms of the counter offer, both the seller and buyer are happy. If not, the second buyer gets a shot at the deal thus giving both buyers a fair chance to purchase the business with neither feeling like a victim.

In my experience, greed, on the part of either buyer or seller, kills more deals than any other negotiating factor. As the saying goes, "Pigs get fat and hogs get butchered." If you want to put the bacon on your table, think "win-win."

CHAPTER EIGHTEEN:

SELL YOUR BUSINESS – PAY NO TAXES

The only two "givens" in life are allegedly death and taxes. Recent medical evidence shows that if we drink more wine and eat more chocolate, we may be able to defer death to some extent. However, taxes seem to dog us even after we've given up the ghost. But not any more!

A little-used, tax-saving vehicle called a Charitable Remainder UniTrust (CRUT) is slowing gaining in popularity and promises to be a panacea for sellers of either a business or real estate who want to avoid post-sale tax woes. Don't be intimidated by the name, this tax-saving method is not as complicated as it appears and it has been scrutinized and approved by the IRS and nationally-recognized financial planners. Here's how it works:

1. Joe Smith, a business owner, wants to retire and have the sale of his business fund his retirement. Prior to putting his business up for sale, Smith donates his business to a charitable trust of his choosing. The costs and technicalities of setting up the trust are often handled by attorneys representing the charity, so there is little out-of-pocket expense to Joe. Joe, acting as the trustee, sells the business to a third party for $1,000,000. Because the business is sold by a charitable trust, the proceeds of the sale are not subject to taxation. This can amount to tax savings in excess of $200,000.

2. Upon consummation of the sale, the proceeds are managed by Smith, who invests the entire $1,000,000 at 5% interest and subsequently receives $50,000 per year as his return on the investment. He is entitled to continue receiving the earnings from this investment until he dies, or in the event he is married, he can elect that these earnings continue until both he and his wife die. At the time of their joint departure, the $1,000,000 trust reverts to Joe's favorite charity.

3. If Joe wants to bequeath an estate to his heirs, a term life insurance policy can be funded from the earnings that will pay $1,000,000 upon his death. Because of the tax-free status of the trust, no estate taxes will be due on the insurance payout, which could save the estate hundreds of thousands of dollars in taxes at the existing tax rate.

4. The fact that Joe Smith is donating $1,000,000 to his favorite charity has some additional pleasant consequences. First, he is entitled to a sizable tax deduction
(calculated using actuarial tables) that can be applied to the taxes due on the income he receives from the trust (or any other sources). This tax deduction can be carried forward for five years to effectively create some tax-free earnings. Secondly, Joe can arrange to have some lasting memorial at his favorite charity, to both comfort his heirs and stimulate other potential donors to do likewise.

A CRUT is only one choice and comes in many variations, including a CRAT (Charitable Remainder Annuity Trust), which will also provide a fixed income for the life of the donor(s).

Sound too good to be true? Believe it! The only way you can't come out ahead with a CRUT or CRAT is if you are so old that you are uninsurable or are so old that you can't look forward to a long life expectancy. However, if you are middle-aged and expect to enjoy your retirement income for several years, a CRUT or CRAT may be just the ticket.

CHAPTER NINETEEN:

GIFTING YOUR BUSINESS TO EMPLOYEES OR FAMILY

Some altruistic business owners feel duty-bound to turn their businesses over to the loyal employees who were responsible, in large part, for the success of the business. While being an admirable consideration, it should be understood that it is a far from easy task. The following three actual examples will expand on this statement.

In the first example, Mr. and Mrs. Entrepreneur decided to retire and leave their business to their employees at no cost. I was asked to present this incredible opportunity to the employees and then to help prepare the Purchase Agreement to complete the sale. I asked an attorney friend, Jim, to assist with the legal work.

In addition to all the normal hard assets of the business, i.e., furniture, fixtures, equipment and inventory, the owners were going to leave $120,000 in operating capital. One other important aspect of the intended transaction was the fact the owners had been more absentee than onsite, which forced the employees to literally run the business as if it were theirs.

When Jim and I met with the twenty-three employees and presented this unprecedented offer, we were met with stone-faced disbelief. Once the importance of the message sunk in, the employees asked for a couple of hours to discuss the situation and make their decision. What I thought would be a slam-dunk acceptance turned into a four hour debate and ultimate refusal. None of the employees were willing to accept the responsibility of operating a going and successful enterprise despite the fact they had virtually been doing so for nearly twenty years. The business was subsequently turned over to the owners' son who ended up closing its doors in less than two years.

In example number two, ma and pa decided to sell their long-time, successful business to their two sons (who had been working in the business for more than five years) and asked me to act as consultant. After providing the owners with an acceptable evaluation, I met with the entire family to discuss the best way to consummate the transaction which was set for four years in the future. The owners were going to sell the business at the purchase price I suggested but on softer than normal terms, i.e., a lower down payment and interest rate, along with a longer payout.

I firmly believe that heirs have to have some "skin in the game" to encourage their best efforts in operating a business. I therefore suggested that the two sons agree to put $10,000 of their $50,000 annual salaries into a down payment fund over the next four years. This would create a down payment of $80,000 for ma and pa to enjoy when the fateful retirement day arrived. It would also create a real incentive for the sons to work as hard as necessary to continue the business's success and follow through on their buyout commitment. After some grousing on the part of the two sons, everyone agreed this was a workable scenario. Four years later, the transfer came off without a hitch.

Made in the USA
San Bernardino, CA
28 September 2015